"In Letters to a Church Girl H
determined ability that was bor
a significant challenge facing young ladies attending church
without being woven into the fabric of God's story. Through a
series of poignant, personal, and practical letters Holly paints a
picture of how the church girl can be transformed to a daughter
of King Jesus. This book is both a call and a challenge for all the
'church girls' to cease being just a consumer of church, to being
truly captivated by her beauty and mission. I can't wait to see
how God will use this message in the coming months and years!"

-Brent Crowe, Vice President of Student
Leadership University, author of *Chasing
Elephants* and *Moments 'til Midnight*

"In her book, Letters to a Church Girl, Holly Ford lays the
groundwork for life 'in Christ' as we read, study and memorize
the Word of God. Addressing the ones who think they have
'heard it all' because they are well versed in 'church', she exposes
how faulty our logic can be when it is not grounded in Scripture.
Written with authenticity and an engaging style, Holly draws us
into the richness of God's Word and helps us build our identity
in Christ. While directed toward the young, these timeless truths
are for every woman!"

-Donna Gaines, Author of *Choose Wisely*,
Live Fully, Founder & President of ARISE2Read,
Bible teacher, pastor's wife, and fellow church girl

"This is a raw and powerful word from God laid on the heart of a
humble and authentic servant! Every woman young and old
should read this book, and I pray that one day my young
daughters will glean from its lifelong lessons!"

-Tonya Greer, pastor's wife, mom of
two daughters, and fellow church girl

"As a young woman in my twenties and a fellow church girl, this book challenged and encouraged me in all the right ways. Since I finished reading, not a day has passed that I haven't thought about all I learned and took away from the chapter Fall in Love with God's Word."

-Erin Rowan, recent college grad
and fellow church girl

"As a high school senior and stereotypical church girl, Holly's book convicted, encouraged, and taught me in ways that I never knew I needed. Her willingness to be honest and open about her past mistakes and challenges has left a lasting impact on me and pushed me to become a better version of myself. I often refer back to her wise words to share with others in my life as they walk through any one of the many challenges young women face."

-Sydney Buckner, high school senior
and fellow church girl

"Holly has a gifted insight into young women and a unique voice with which to share life lessons from both Scripture and her own life. She speaks to them in their language, appeals to their hearts with clear truths, and teaches them examples that are real life."

-Pam Rector, teacher
and fellow church girl

LETTERS TO A

Church Girl

LETTERS TO A

Church Girl

HOLLY FORD

She Delights

All Scripture quotations, unless otherwise indicated, are taken from the Holy Bible, New International Version®, NIV®. Copyright ©1973, 1978, 1984, 2011 by Biblica, Inc.™ Used by permission of Zondervan. All rights reserved worldwide. www.zondervan.com

The "NIV" and "New International Version" are trademarks registered in the United States Patent and Trademark Office by Biblica, Inc.™

Cover Design: Trenn Carnes
Cover Photo: Morgan Watson Photography

ISBN: 978-1-7358718-0-6

Library of Congress Control Number: 2020920090

Printed in the United States of America

First Edition 2020

Shout-Outs

Thank you, Jesus, for the abundant life I have in you. You remind me daily that your grace is sufficient, and you are able to do so much more that we could ever ask or imagine. I love you.

Wes, thank you for the countless hours you've spent dedicating your time to this book and ministry. Thank you for taking "I Do" to a whole new level. I wouldn't want to do life with anyone else.

Jaxon and Annabeth, thank you for being my biggest cheerleaders and for your patience every time I had to say "no" for the cause of this book. I don't deserve to be your mom but am so thankful God allowed me to anyway.

To all those who read this manuscript, I cannot thank you enough for your support. I'm grateful to God to have you in my corner.

Pam, thank you for putting up with my slouchy writing style while editing this book and for taking so much of your time to invest in me. You are just fabulous!

To my pastors at Red Bank and their wives, your support and encouragement have meant the world to me. It's a pleasure to serve alongside you all.

To my family, thank you for raising me in a home that loved Jesus. Your words of affirmation throughout this whole process and my life so far have always been encouraging. I love you all.

This Is for You

To all the church girls I have been given the undeserving privilege to pour into, this book is for you. Thank you for enduring my frail attempts to lead long before I was ready and for allowing me to grow alongside of you. If this book finds you still in student ministry, in college, or even with a family of your own, I pray you live in the truth of God's Word and find your delight in the Lord alone.

To my own church girl, Annabeth, this book is also for you. I pray you love the Lord with all your heart, soul, mind, and strength. May you be strong. May you be independent. And, may you delight in the only one you'll ever need – Jesus. I love you, lil' girl.

Truths

Introduction

Dear Self,

You were a church girl. You had heard it all before. Love your neighbor. Be kind and compassionate. Forgive others. Go, therefore. You had heard of Noah and the ark, Moses, David and Goliath, the calling of the twelve, Jesus and the Samaritan woman, the resurrection, Paul's journeys, and even the story of a talking donkey. You had accepted Christ as your Savior. You've gone to church camps, conventions, and revivals. You've participated in Bible studies, VBS, and True Love Waits. You sang in the choir and on the worship team. But it just didn't click. It didn't stick. All of the lessons, all of the stories, all of the sermons and songs and service are only jaded responses to your religion. Why did it take so long for you to understand? Why did it take so long to become important? Why did you wait until you were ankle deep in adulthood before you allowed all these truths to make an impact on your daily life? Self, you wasted so much time.

Sincerely,

Holly

Still a Church Girl

Dear Church Girl,

Maybe you're like me. You're a church girl who has heard it all and learned it all, but it just hasn't really stuck. I'm hoping you read these letters well before your thirties are knocking at your door. That's how long it took me. It took almost thirty years for me to grasp some of these truths and learn what it truly means to live them out. You see, I underestimated myself. It never occurred to me that I was capable of living these out in my younger years. Society was telling me the same thing it is telling you. You're too young. Live it up while you can. You're not supposed to care until you're older. You've got all the time in the world. And I believed it.

My husband and I have been in student ministry for over 16 years. We've learned so much about the issues, difficulties, joys, and triumphs of the next generation. What's hot and what's not, fashion, technology and even slang have all changed from year to year, but one element seems to remain constant -- potential. And, we are very passionate about compelling young men and women to see their potential now and not wait until they are older with careers and families of their own.

The young people my husband and I have had the privilege to mentor come from all different backgrounds, families, and social statuses. They have very unique personalities, and we have watched students fail many times. But, oh, how we have also watched them succeed. We have watched a couple of young people lead an entire student ministry to take responsibility for the care and love of a fellow student with special needs, an action which influenced the church as a whole. We have witnessed a student take it upon himself to learn the sound and technology skills needed for our church so he could help with that ministry, without pay. We've seen students overcome incredibly difficult socioeconomic odds and rise to reach their potential.

We have heard countless stories of young men and women who are using their schools and universities as mission fields and having Gospel conversations with their peers and professors. We've watched students work hard, intentionally preparing for their future. Futures that include making a difference in their colleges, becoming mothers and fathers, serving in our Armed Forces, and becoming police officers, teachers, preachers, engineers, coaches, and businessmen and women. They are full of potential. You are full of potential.

For three years now, we've taken some of our students who make up our Student Leadership Team to Orlando for a leadership training conference called Student Leadership University (SLU). We take young people who are serious about making changes now that will better their future. SLU is an organization whose mission is equipping and enabling young people to see their potential and prepare them now for what God's plan is for their lives. They value young people and their ability to learn to use their potential now. And, so do I.

During one of our seminars at SLU 101, the speaker and vice president, Brent Crowe, Ph.D., was describing to us how church kids go on these emotional roller coasters. We do all the Bible studies and go to all the camps and never miss worship on Sundays. But the truths never stick, and we are chasing our tails. People do not follow those who are going in circles. He said, "At some point, it's got to stick."[1] Those words hit me so hard. As I looked at the students who came with us, I thought, "I wish I would have figured out how to make it stick when I was a younger woman. I wish I would have learned practical ways to allow these truths to impact everyday life." As I looked at the young women around the room, I thought, "Are you listening? Do you understand that you don't have to wait? Do you know you can make it stick now?"

We need to wake up. Church girl, you need to wake up. Look in the mirror. It's time you start to see yourself for what you really are - the present. True, you are the future. You are the future America. You are the future church, the future ambassadors for Jesus Christ. But you are not just the future, you are the present. It's time for you to realize your potential and allow yourself to be taught and equipped now instead of waiting until your yesteryear is a distant memory. And, trust me, that will happen sooner than you think.

In the conclusion to the Sermon on the Mount, Jesus tells us the parable of the wise and foolish builders. He says:

Therefore, everyone who hears these words of mine and puts them into practice is like a wise man who built his house on the rock. The rain came down, the streams rose, and the winds blew and beat against that house; yet it did not fall, because it had its foundation on the rock.
Matthew 7:24-27

We know the other builder in the story. He hears the words but doesn't apply them to his life. This foolish man builds his house on the sand, and when the storm came, it went crashing down. Both were builders. Both the wise and foolish man heard the same word. They were taught the same lessons, and they probably attended the same Bible study and sang with each other in the praise band. The difference? One of them actually built his life on what he heard and made these words his foundation. The other one only heard them.

Whether you are waiting on results of your ACT's or trying to get through varsity basketball, these letters are for you. If you are drowning in your freshman year of college or ready to face the career world, they're for you. Planning your wedding? Starting a family? Yes, even you. Even if you are pushing thirty and just feel like you've missed something. These letters are for you, too.

Church girl, don't spend the next 15 years building your life on shifting sands. Lay your solid foundation now. I hope these letters encourage you to look for the potential that you have now. I hope they equip you to understand these truths now. I hope these letters challenge you to search for things that need to change and inspire you to take these seemingly clichéd lessons and allow them to truly impact your life -- now. It's time for it to stick.

Dear Church Girl, Know Who You Are

Who are you? Seems like a simple question, but I don't just mean your name. I mean who are you? Are you a sister, an athlete, a techie, a VSCO girl, a plain ol' average Joe? Like me, maybe you've asked yourself this question many times, or maybe this is a new question you've never tried to answer before. Take a moment to answer it below. Who are you?

_____

_____

_____

_____

_____

_____

When we are asked this question, especially by unfamiliar people, our answer tends to sound something like this:

My name is Holly, and I have a wonderful husband and two beautiful children. We live in Chattanooga where I work as a school nurse. I like to sing, and I love avocados.

I know there would be variations to my bio, but we would essentially describe it the same way. I'm Brittany and am attending such and such college with a dog named Spot. I work at Starbucks and like to watch Netflix. Or, I'm Rebecca. I have a newborn at home and live with my parents. I am looking for the right job but love to read during my free time. Different lives, different stories, different people, but we all answer this question the same way. We tell who we are by giving our names and details about family, job, school, and hobbies. Some of our bios will be long, others will be short and sweet. But, ladies, it took me way too long to figure out none of that has anything to do with who I am. Oh, I have so much to say to you about this. These things, these people, these tasks do not give you your meaning or define who you are.

But you are a chosen people, a royal priesthood, a holy nation, God's special possession, that you may declare the praises of him who called you out of darkness into his wonderful light.
I Peter 2:9

At the beginning of this verse, we read this word: but. This means something was said before that will give this verse more meaning and context. Let's look at it together. 1 Peter 2:4-8 says:

As you come to him, the living Stone – rejected by humans but chosen by God and precious to him – you also, like living stones, are being built into a spiritual house to be a holy priesthood, offering spiritual sacrifices acceptable to God through Jesus Christ. For in Scripture it says: "See, I lay a stone in Zion, a chosen and precious cornerstone, and the one who trusts in him will never be put to shame." Now to you who believe, this stone is precious. But to those who do not believe, "The stone the builders rejected has become the cornerstone," and "A stone that caused people to stumble and a rock that makes them fall." They stumble because they disobey the message – which is also what they were destined for.

These verses tell us that Jesus is the living stone, the cornerstone, rejected by humans. But Peter tells us that this Cornerstone was chosen by God and precious to Him. Don't miss this. Peter goes on to say that we (Christians) are stones being built into a spiritual house, and we are heirs to the throne and precious to the Lord as well, just as Jesus is. Wow. We are precious to the Lord as Jesus is precious to the Lord. Jesus refers to himself as the chief cornerstone. One would normally say that the cornerstone was the most important stone before laying any foundation. However, my friend, Bill, helped me understand this a little better. Bill is a retired engineer and missionary. He has quite the spiritual resume. And, yes, I realize he may seem to be a little old for me to call him my friend, but he is my friend. I have lots of old friends. It makes me smarter and kinder. You should have lots of old friends too. I'm digressing. Bill explained to me that in 1 Corinthians 3:11, we are told that Christ is the foundation. Then, we read in 1 Peter that he is also the cornerstone. Turns out, even in the times these were written, the cornerstone would have been placed after the foundation. And Jesus was both! This cornerstone determined the design and the structure of the entire building. It was set carefully in the foundation wall and was often placed in the corner from which all other building elements are located. And we are part of the stones or elements that make up this building, His Church. To those of us who are believers, this Cornerstone is precious. It is life. It is everything. But to those who do not believe, this cornerstone is rejected, ultimately leading to their eternal fall. And, this is scary news. This is heartbreaking news that those who don't believe will fall and spend an eternity without God. And, then we have this word *but*, and it changes everything. It changes who we are. It changes our purpose. It changes the destiny of those who believe. But.

You know, I've been trying for years to get my husband to do a sermon series with our students entitled "I like big buts and I cannot lie," because there are so many life-altering buts in God's Word. Buts that change the course of history. Buts that give meaning and purpose, and, in this case, buts that give us our identity.

But you are a chosen people, a royal priesthood, a holy nation, God's special possession, that you may declare the praises of him who called you out of darkness into his wonderful light.
I Peter 2:9

If we are not careful, we can take this verse and make it about what it is not. We can put on our crowns and prance around, never fully understanding what we must put aside in order to grasp its true meaning. There are certain lies about who we are that need to be put to rest, and before we can know who we really are, we must first know who we are not. We have to understand the identity crisis in which we are in the middle. We must identify and recognize the deception surrounding us and lying to us about our identity, especially as young women.

We are women. We do a lot of things. A lot is expected of us. And, if you are just now beginning to embrace womanhood from girlhood, we welcome you with open arms and a lot of hooks. Hooks for the many hats you will be expected to wear, sometimes all at once. We do so much, and while we are busy doing many good things, I want us to realize that our identity is not wrapped up in what we do.

We Are Not What We Do

Wherever you live, wherever you work, whatever accomplishments you achieve, whatever friends you have, whoever you marry, whatever career you choose, or whatever amount of things on your to do list for any given day does not define who you are. And, don't we get so caught up in doing? Our society sometimes demands our busyness to define who we are. We make our accomplishments tell us our worth. But what if we get to the place where we can't do those things? What if our friends stop talking to us? What if our boyfriend likes someone else? What if we are not accepted into the college we've dreamed of attending since we were young? What about when we lose our job? Or lose our physical ability to even get out of bed? Do we become nothing? Is our identity suddenly lost? And, it's not that doing these things are bad. There is nothing wrong with furthering your education, building close friendships, relaxing in your vacation home on the beach or setting sky-high goals for your career. These are all great things, but we cannot let these things tell us who we are and what we are worth. We are not what we do.

We Are Not What Others Say We Are

Some of ya'll need to hear this. Say it with me: We are not what others say we are. Whether good or bad. We don't have to think too hard to remember hurtful things others have said about us, intentional or unintentional. Words that sting and stay with us.

I grew up my entire life with people telling me what kind of person I was. You see, I can speak two languages very well. I speak English and Sarcasm. Oh, c'mon, I know I'm not the only one with sarcasm as their second language. I'm very fluent, and everyone would always say, "That's just Holly." Because of what they would say, I thought I had an excuse for the way I treated people. I had an excuse for the way I would rant over government or politics. I had an excuse for the way I spoke the truth but did it in a not so loving way. It was just the way I was, so I had a good excuse for my actions and attitude, right? And this happened so much growing up that I started to believe it. I began to believe that I was just a sarcastic know-it-all who spoke harshly and just couldn't help it because that's just who I was. One day, it occurred to me that I had spent many years defining myself based on what others said about me and who they thought I was. Oh, the power of our words, friends. The power of our words, sisters, students, wives, moms. Our words have the ability to define or at least manipulate, and early in my adult years, I had to make a choice. I had to believe that I was not defined by what others said about who I was, and, clearly, I had a lot of work to do to change my behavior. You are not who others say you are. You may have had people tell you that you're worthless. Useless. That you'll never measure up. You're not smart. You'll never make it and neither will your marriage. You're a terrible mom. You're too young to understand. The question is this: Are you seeking your identity from what someone else says about you? Or, are you looking for your identity in what someone else thinks or says of you? Let me tell you, ladies, I am not who they say I am. I am who Jesus says I am. And so are you. He says with Him, you can do it. He says you are precious. He says you're beautiful. He says you are useful to His kingdom work. He says you are not too young. And, He says you are worth dying for. You are not what others say you are.

We Are Not What Society Tells Us We Should Be

Teddy Roosevelt once said, "Comparison is the thief of joy."[2] It really is, at least one of them. Society wants you to believe that your identity is wrapped up in many things. Your identity is wrapped up in how attractive you are. How ambitious you are. How wealthy you are. Your identity is defined by the career you choose or the job you hold. And what is our standard? Who else do we look at to tell us who we are, other than those around us? You see, what we do is get on Instagram or Snapchat or Twitter or whatever social media we choose, and we scroll through profiles full of picture-perfect young women who are masking their hurts, their failures, their true identity behind their photos. And, we only see the filtered perfect. We see a young woman who has the most beautiful and symmetrical face and the perfect body, and we count the endless likes on her bikini selfies. All of a sudden, we think we are not beautiful enough, and we buy a gym membership and eat only spinach for lunch. We never see how she struggles to keep friends. We see a girl and her attractive boyfriend and think "hashtag goals," and we feel less than because we don't have that kind of relationship. We don't see her history of abuse. We see the woman graduating top of her class when we have worked so hard for grades that are average. We never see her loneliness. We see the popular girl who is liked by everyone and is leader of her sorority when we still live at home and eat dinner with the family every night. We don't see her terrible relationship with her parents. We see the women who are working their way up the career ladder while we are still working the fitting rooms at Marshall's. We never see their failures. And, we think we are not enough. We don't measure up. We will only just be average. We begin to compare ourselves, and what we see on social media becomes our standard of who we are supposed to be.

But, listen carefully. If you are in Christ and living under someone else's identity, you are living a lie. We lose our identity because we become someone we really aren't, and we strive to be someone else. This steals our joy. It steals our purpose. It steals our confidence. It steals our true identity.

We Are Not Our Circumstances

Past or Present. Our identity is not wrapped up in our situations. Our surroundings. We all come from different backgrounds. Some of us may come from the other side of the tracks, so to speak. But we can't put our identity in that because all of that can change. Even our personalities, our hobbies, and what we like change. I was once a girl who wore overalls and a ponytail at any given time, watched NASCAR, and could spit farther than most boys. But I changed. My personality changed. My hobbies changed. Even where I lived changed. We often let our past situations become a huge part of our identity. We let it define who we are and even define our future, never breaking the cycle. We do this with our current circumstances as well. But people change. Circumstances change, whether it be losing your friend group, failing a class, a bad break up, switching career paths, or losing your job. But Jesus never changes. He stays the same, no matter what changes around us. We cannot keep letting our circumstances tell us who we are. Because even though our conditions change, we are still who He says we are.

We Are Not Our Sin

Sins from your past, sins you are caught in the middle of, sins you have yet to commit…they do not define who you are. This is a big one. You are not your lust. You are not your greed. You are not your pride. You are not your addictions. You are a child of God who has accepted the free gift of grace. And, you are forgiven. We have got to let go of the past, repent of our present sinfulness, and not live in fear of the future mistakes we are going to make. Rest in the forgiveness of Jesus, friends. You are not your sin.

Do you know why we can't find our identity in what we do or what others say or in someone else's life or in our circumstances or even in our sin? Because we can't find our identity in a place we don't belong to begin with. We do not belong here. We are visiting. Passing through. There's so much more in store for us than what this place has to offer, and Jesus is the only one who has earned the right to give us our identity.

So, now we know what our identity is not. We've put lies to rest and uncovered some myths about our identity. Let's dive deep into what our identity actually is in Christ. Let's read it again.

But you are a chosen people, a royal priesthood, a holy nation, God's special possession, that you may declare the praises of him who called you out of darkness into his wonderful light.
1 Peter 2:9

We Are a Chosen People

The Greek for chosen people is derived from the word eklegó meaning "to pick out, choose."[3] This means God picked us out for Himself. We are chosen. If I were to ask you if you choose God, everyone reading this would emphatically agree that, yes, we choose God. We choose Jesus. But may I suggest that we didn't choose Jesus. We may choose to follow Him, but He actually chose us. But aren't we so arrogant to make it about us? To think, "Lord, I'm going to give my life to you. Aren't you proud of me?" The Bible tells us that we are God's chosen people, and that means we are deeply and personally selected into the family of God.

Have you ever been the last one picked? You know, you're playing ball or any other kind of team sports. Or, maybe you're playing a board game, like trivia, and it just ain't your thing. Or, maybe you can remember in middle school when your classmates would pick who was going to be on their team during the study guide review game to earn extra points on your test. And, you were the last one standing? Being picked last hurts. It stings. It makes us feel less-than. Not good enough.

But think about this. An almighty God who is powerful enough to create the universe with stars and galaxies and massive enough to create a world perfectly formed for human survival, who is great enough to part seas, make dry bones come alive, cause walls to crumble, and the sun to stand still, a God who is big enough to heal the sick and raise the dead, a God who is selfless enough to send His own Son to die to rescue us but jealous enough to want His creation all for Himself, a God whose mercy and forgiveness is endless. That God chose you. That God created you so that He could live within you. That God chases after you and says, "I want You." We, sisters in Christ, are chosen.

And, the beauty of it is, we didn't have to be good enough. We didn't have to be the best. We didn't have to prove anything. Jesus did all of that for us on the cross. And God knew full well when He created us that we were not enough. But He loved us so much that He sent someone who was enough to take our place and give us our identity. He chose us. We are chosen.

We Are a Royal Priesthood

My daughter, Annabeth, used to love to dress up. She would put on a princess dress, her crown, and high heels and would prance around the house. But the funny thing is, Annabeth never had a desire to be a princess. She would wear her princess attire to play dates, daycare, and even the mall. Inevitably, someone would tell her that she was the most beautiful princess they had ever seen, to which she would reply with all the sass she could muster up, "I am NOT a princess. I'm the QUEEN." But, whether princess or queen, she loved her crown, and I think we all can relate. We like this royal part, the crown, and everything else that comes with being a princess, right? But I want us to try to put a little extra emphasis on the second part of this phrase. Priesthood.

What does this mean? What is a priesthood? The Greek for this simply means "the office of the priest."[4] So, what does the office of the priest entail? It was the job of the priest to reflect the holiness of God and of the High Priest. Hebrews 7:23-27 says:

Now there have been many of those priests, since death prevented them from continuing in office; but because Jesus lives forever, he has a permanent priesthood. Therefore, he is able to save completely those who come to God through him, because he always lives to intercede for them. Such a high priest truly meets our need – one who is holy, blameless, pure, set apart from sinners, exalted above the heavens. Unlike the other high priests, he does not need to offer sacrifices day after day, first for his own sins, and then for the sins of the people. He sacrificed for their sins once for all when he offered himself.

Wow! Jesus Christ is our permanent High Priest because of the sacrifice He made on the cross. If we are now a royal priesthood and we are to reflect the holiness of the High Priest, then that means we are to reflect Jesus Christ. You see, there's a certain weight that this word priesthood carries. These verses we just read tell us that Jesus, our

High Priest, is holy, blameless, pure, and set apart from sinners. But are we? So far, we have made ourselves feel good with the truth. Sometimes the truth feels good. Other times it just plain steps on our toes. And, that's what this word priesthood does. We want to make this about the pretty crowns we wear because we are princesses, but that's not what this is about at all. We are priests of the King. But are we reflecting the High Priest? Church girls, could we examine our lives for just a moment and ask for a revelation from the Lord about this? Lord, show us areas of our life that we are not reflecting you! Can we do that? Are we bold enough to do that?

It was also the job of the priest to make sacrifices. Now we just read that we do not have to do this to atone our sins anymore because Jesus' blood is good enough to cover it all for everyone forever. So, what is it that we sacrifice now? When we have questions, there's no better place to look than God's Word. We are told in Romans 12:1:

Therefore, I urge you, brothers and sisters, in view of God's mercy, to offer your bodies as a living sacrifice, holy and pleasing to God – this is your true and proper worship.

Did y'all hear that? We are still commanded to sacrifice, only we sacrifice ourselves, holy and pleasing to God. That's what we sacrifice. As part of the priesthood, we, sisters in Christ, are called to reflect Jesus and sacrifice ourselves for His glory. What we want, what we choose, how we want to live, we sacrifice all of that to Him. Not for Him, we aren't doing Him any favors. God doesn't need this, but we sacrifice it to Him because of the mercy He has shown us.

There is another responsibility of the priest that we read about. It was the job of the priest to intercede on behalf of the people. Jesus intercedes for us, but we are to also intercede for others. 1 Timothy 2:1-2 says:

I urge, then, first of all, that petitions, prayers, intercession and thanksgiving be made for all people – for kings and all those in authority....

We are supposed to be interceding for ALL people. Even the kings and authorities. That means we are interceding for that president or congressman we don't like or that professor who is out to get us or that pastor we just don't care for. We are to be interceding for the bully, that girl who hates us, and the boy that broke our heart. We are to be interceding for our friends, our family, the lost, the saved, and even our enemies. Ladies, we know the One who has all the answers, and we have the overwhelming privilege to petition to Him whenever we want. Because of the blood of the Lamb, He is always readily available for us to approach His throne of grace boldly and confidently, like it tells us in Hebrews 4:16. It is the job of the High Priest, Jesus Christ, to intercede for us, so it is the job of those in the royal priesthood to intercede for others.

We want to make this about wearing a crown and being a princess, but we forget the humbling responsibility we have as part of the priesthood. Church girls, we are going to throw our crowns at the feet of Jesus anyway! We are a chosen people. We are a royal priesthood.

We Are a Holy Nation

The word holy means "separated to God."[5] We are a people who are set apart and different from the world. Let's explore this word holy for a moment. I think it's important for us to walk this fine line together for just a minute. Yes, holiness does mean that we are separated from ordinary or wicked, but it also means we are set apart for God's purposes. It's both, not either/or. Just because we are refraining from wicked things, does not automatically mean we are about doing the will of God either. Our holiness is the very reason we needed salvation. We were terrible people, stuck deep in sin and a holy and perfect God could not be in relationship with us because of it. Oswald Chambers said this:

God has only one intended destiny for mankind – holiness. His only goal is to produce saints. God is not some eternal blessing-machine for people to use, and he did not come to save us out of pity – he came to save us because he created us to be holy.[6]

Ladies, we were created to be set apart for God's use!
But the fine line is this: Holiness is not about being moral. Our goal should not be to check off our list of moral standards. Our goal is to be in Christ and to live like it! And, we do this through obedience. We read the Hall of Faith in Hebrews 11 and see these tremendous patriarchs and examples of those who obeyed by faith, not because that's what would bring them salvation, but because they

loved and trusted the Lord so much that it actually showed. They loved the Lord, and desire burned inside of them to obey. The same goes with us. We are saved by the blood of Jesus Christ, and it gives us a burning desire to put our faith into action by being obedient and surrendering to the will of the Father. Pursue Jesus, ladies, not your checklist. Holiness is about our relationship, not how closely we follow our checklist of do's and don'ts.

I used to fall into this trap, and it was only several years ago that I realized I was working myself to death for no reason. I suddenly decided to become transparent. I decided that my long list of what I should be doing wasn't the point at all. Attending church three times a week did not make me any holier than the next girl. Accidentally cursing did not make me any less holy than the next girl either. It's only through Christ's work on the cross that a Christian is holy. But God is asking so much more of us in these words "holy nation" than just obedience and following the rules. We can live our lives fairly "holy" if we happen to be good at following the rules and, thus, never know our identity, never know who we are or, worse, never know who He is. You see, God wants all of us, every single part of us, so much that He has marked our very identity. Holiness is about being and living in Christ because it's only in Him where our true holiness can dwell, which brings me to the last part of our identity that Peter talks about.

We Are His Special Possession

This possessive word used here is so incredible because the Greek definition for its usage here is "into, towards,"[7] as if towards a purpose or goal. His = being in Christ so as to accomplish our purpose. He does not merely own us, but we are in Him! And His Spirit dwells in us. This word possession doesn't just mean He owns us but that He acquired us. He paid for us. He bought us. In an ugly, ugly way. And, we know that it was only through the blood of Jesus that He acquired us. So, basically, He bought me, an uncommon and peculiar human being to live in Him and fulfill His purpose. Wow. If that doesn't make you feel special, I don't know what will.

My husband, Wes, shows that he loves me in all kinds of ways. Ya'll, I'm so sorry I took the best guy. I know that was very selfish of me, but it is what it is. I made a special gift for him on one of our anniversaries. I gave him a list of 101 reasons why I love him, and I had it framed it. The list included things like letting me put my cold feet on him, taking the shopping cart back, fixing me cereal at night, and providing for our family. The funny thing is, this gift not only showed why I love him, but it really showed how he loves me. These things make me feel so special. And I can read over this and never have to guess if Wes loves me because of the many things on this list. But there is still nothing he can do that would prove his love for me like dying for me. Dying in my place. Saving me from an eternity in hell. Wiping my sins clean. Not even the best husband in the world can do that, but an almighty God can. And, He loved us that much.

We are a chosen people, a royal priesthood, a holy nation and His special possession. But why? We've read about our identity in the first part of this verse, but in the latter part, we find our purpose.

But you are a chosen people, a royal priesthood, a holy nation, God's special possession, that you may declare the praises of him who called you out of darkness into his wonderful light.
I Peter 2:9

We were created to declare the praises of our God. Even in Isaiah 43:21, God tells us that *"the people, I formed for myself, that they may proclaim my praise."* But look at our motive, look at why we are proclaiming His praise -- because we have been called out of darkness into his wonderful light. Young women, this is our story! Our story is, "I was this, but now I'm this." I was headed for this but now I'm headed for this. We have an I was but now story! I was in darkness, now I'm in the wonderful light of Christ. All of our stories may be unique and very different, how we came into a relationship with Christ may not look the same at all, but, rest assured, Church girls, we all have an I was but now story!

And the word proclaim does not mean to whisper. It means to declare. We read this same word in John when Mary Magdalene comes to the tomb. After realizing the tomb of Jesus is empty, she meets a man and soon realizes it is Jesus! He's been raised to life! He has conquered the grave! And John 20:18 says:

Mary Magdalene went to the disciples with the news: "I have seen the Lord!" and she told them that he had said these things to her.

The root word used here for told is the same word used for proclaim in 1 Peter. It is aggelos, and it means "to announce, declare."[8] Don't you like that? Mary was announcing the good news. Declaring the truth. We are announcing the good news of Jesus Christ, and this is our purpose. We were created for this. To be in relationship with Jesus, proclaim His praises, and share our story.

Oh, young women, who are you? I know you've asked yourself that question many times. Who are you? If you haven't been able to answer that question truthfully, can I ask you to examine your heart? It may be the reason you can't seem to find your identity in Christ is because you are not in Him at all. If this is you, please stop reading right now and turn to *I Was but Now* at the end of this book.

Some of you may need to surrender your lives to Christ today. It doesn't matter if you are 19 or 99. Today is the day of salvation. You may very well be thinking, "Holly, I don't think I've truly made that choice to wholeheartedly surrender my life and my wants and purpose over to Jesus." I don't care if you are a newbie to this church thing or if you are a church girl like myself, I want the best for you. And, there is no better best than to know Jesus personally and surrender to him. Please, please, if this is you, don't wait. Find someone, talk to them. Today is the day for your salvation. Jesus chose you, so follow Him.

Some of you church girls are young women of God, true followers of Jesus, but somewhere along the way you've let your identity be wrapped up in your past or what others think of you or what society tells you to be. Or, maybe you have lost your holiness amongst your checklist. You've made a mental list of dos and don'ts and try to follow them to a tee, all while missing out on building your relationship with Jesus and living in Him. Some of you may have forgotten your purpose. You've made it about wearing your crown and riding it out. You think you are secure in your salvation, so no need to worry about anything else. And, some of you church girls have neglected your true purpose to declare the good news, to share your stories, and to have those intentional Gospel conversations.

Examine your heart. Demand the lies be laid to rest. Take up the truth of who you are and believe it with everything you've got. Shout it from the rooftops and live it in the lowest valleys. You are chosen. You are a royal priesthood. You are a holy nation. You are His special possession. Now, go and live like it.

Know who you are,

Holly

Make it Stick, Church Girl

1. Which part of your identity do you struggle with the most? A chosen people, a royal priesthood, a holy nation, or God's special possession? Why?

2. Which lies have you believed about your identity?

3. Who are you most likely to compare yourself to and why?

4. As I mentioned before, our purpose is to glorify the Lord and point others to Him. We do this by sharing our story. Share your story below.

Don't know what sharing your story looks like? Check out my story in *I Was but Now* at the end of the book.

5. What are some areas of your life that may need repentance? Areas that you may not be reflecting our High Priest, Jesus Christ?

Dear Church Girl, Fall in Love with God's Word

I love all my friends. I love to hang out with them. I love to worship with them. I love to serve with them. I love to encourage them and be encouraged by them. They really do mean the world to me. But my best friend is my husband. He's my jam. He is always available and uplifting. He's good-looking and flat out funny. I love to laugh with him, and there's no one else I'd rather spend time with than him. He truly is my main squeeze! However, I have taken a new delight in something else these past few years. I have this newer relationship that has brought me more joy and meaning than any other, including my husband. It's a relationship that has held me, motivated me, and loved me with a love that's unexplainable. I have fallen in love with

God's Word. And I'm still falling. Hard. But it shouldn't have taken this long. I've had a relationship with Jesus since 8th grade. I grew up in a Christian home and attended church regularly. Why in the world did it take until well into my twenties to really delight in the Word of God? My prayer is that this chapter compels you to use the Bible the way it is meant to be used and understand the implications if we neglect it. But my prayer is also that you would fall in love with the Word of God and make it your best friend.

All Means All

All Scripture is God-breathed and is useful for teaching, rebuking, correcting and training in righteousness, so that the servant of God may be thoroughly equipped for every good work.
2 Timothy 3:16-17

My pastor, Dr. Sam Greer, reads these verses and says, "All means ALL." And that's exactly what it means. Every word is not only inspired by God but is also useful. Every single word. Not part of it. Not just the verses we like. Not just what is convenient for us. Not just the New Testament. Not just the Old Testament. All means all. God-breathed means that all scripture is inspired by God. Peter tells us that "...*prophecy never had its origin in the human will, but prophets, though human, spoke from God as they were carried along by the Holy Spirit*" (2 Peter 1:21). Through the Holy Spirit, God spoke to the prophets and writers of His Word. Therefore, the Bible is inspired by God Himself.

This is huge because if the Bible were not written by God, it loses all credibility. Are we to actually believe absolute truth from mere humans? Believing that Scripture came from God Himself is foundational to trusting in what it says. And, this takes faith.

God's Word tells us it is useful for all kinds of things, and we will discuss many of them in this chapter. But, for now, we are going to focus on how it is useful for training in righteousness by teaching, rebuking and correcting. To help explain how it is used for this, allow me to introduce you to Kate, Sydney and Chelsea. Humor me.

The Scenario

Kate, Sydney and Chelsea are part of a small group that meets once a week along with two other young women. On this particular Tuesday night, Kate, who is often late and unorganized, shows up 15 minutes late and has not completed her Bible study workbook for the week. After ending their meeting in prayer, everyone leaves except Sydney and Chelsea, who stick around to chat. "Kate never does her workbook. She just isn't taking this seriously like the rest of us," Sydney says. "I know, right? And that new boyfriend she has is bad news. That could be a big reason why she doesn't have time for Bible study. She's always with him," Chelsea replies. "He's not really any better than the last one. Another problem is that she is so all over the place, she doesn't make enough time for Bible study. If she would just get organized and learn some time management skills, already," Sydney insists. Both girls nod in affirmation and go home.

Teaching

A large reason we need to know what scripture says is because it teaches us what is right. Romans 15:4 says, *"For everything that was written in the past was written to teach us"* so that we learn endurance for this life and have hope for what's to come. God's Word is truth. The laws, decrees, promises, and commands given to us are to teach us to live a life pleasing to the Father. It teaches us His will.

Let's refer back to our scenario. Sydney and Chelsea obviously need to look to Scripture to teach them a thing or two. Studying Scripture would reveal to them that they are to speak words that are *"...only what is helpful for building others up..."* (Ephesians 4:29). It would also reveal that the *"...prudent hold their tongues"* (Proverbs 10:19) and that *"Whoever would foster love covers over an offense..."* (Proverbs 17:9). Not to mention the whole *"Love your neighbor"* thing (Matthew 22:34-40). These verses are examples of what God wants to teach Sydney, Chelsea, and us about the right way to speak and the right things to talk about. That means it is His will for us to speak productive words to help others, to love someone in such a way that their offenses are covered by it, and to love Kate as we want to be loved. God's Word teaches us.

Rebuking

This may seem unusual, but I love to study the original language of God's Word. The Greek word used for rebuking is elegcho. It simply means "show him his fault."[9] God uses scripture to reveal our sin to us. We have to recognize our sin in order to repent. God shines a flashlight on our sin, so to speak, bringing our wrong doings to light. There are several truths in God's Word that would help reveal and rebuke the problems with Sydney and Chelsea's conversation. Paul wrote for us to *"...not let any unwholesome talk come out of your mouths..."* (Ephesians 4:29). And, take a look at what God tells us in James 1:26 about taming our tongues:

Those who consider themselves religious and yet do not keep a tight rein on their tongues deceive themselves, and their religion is worthless.

Proverbs 16:28 says that *"A perverse person stirs up conflict, and a gossip separates close friends."* All of these Scriptures, as well as others, are examples of God's Word rebuking, or shedding light, on our sin. It tells us what is wrong, so we know what is obedient to our Father.

Correcting

The Greek word for correcting comes from anorthoo, which means to "to set straight."[10] The Bible not only sheds light on what is right and wrong but also tells us how to correct it. Now, this is two-fold, so stay with me. First of all, the Bible tells us what to do to make amends in the moment. For instance, James 5:16 teaches us to "...*confess your sins to each other and pray for each other so that you may be healed.*" Sydney and Chelsea should make an apology to each other, confessing that they never should have been talking about Kate. Next, the Bible says they should pray for each other. Memorizing 2 Timothy 2:16 might help them to avoid gossiping about Kate in the future. It says, "*Avoid godless chatter, because those who indulge in it will become more and more ungodly.*" Scripture memorization is vital for avoiding temptation. We will talk about this more later. The Bible tells us how to correct the situation in the moment, or here on earth, but it also tells us how to correct our sin for eternity. God's Word says, "*if we confess our sins, He is faithful and just and will forgive us our sins and purify us from all unrighteousness*" (1 John 1:9). It also tells us that "*Godly sorrow brings repentance that leads to salvation...*" (2 Corinthians 7:10). We accept God's gift of salvation by repenting. This is how we correct our sin problem once and for all. If you have not yet repented and made the decision to follow Christ, stop reading this chapter and skip over to *I Was but Now* at the end of this book to hear how to become a Christ follower.

And there you have it. According to 2 Timothy 3:16-17, God's Word is useful for teaching, rebuking and correcting. Now, it may seem like I've left "training in righteousness" out, but this is intentional. All three of the uses we've talked about so far are ways we are trained in righteousness. God uses scripture to teach us what is right, rebuke what is wrong, and tell us how to correct, which is how we are trained in righteousness. So, what is the point of being trained in righteousness? I'm so glad you asked!

OK, so I'm going to break out some Greek one more time, but, hey, this whole chapter is talking about the importance of Scripture. So, I totally believe giving you the Greek origins of these words is permissible. The Greek word we are looking at here is paideuo, which means "to train children."[11] In other words, the Bible gives us instruction so that we will grow in truth. We are not meant to stay baby Christians. We are meant to grow and flourish in Word and Truth. Hebrews 6:1 says:

Therefore, let us move beyond the elementary teachings about Christ and be taken forward to maturity, not laying again the foundation of repentance from acts that lead to death, and of faith in God.

God's Word will teach, rebuke, and correct in order to train us in righteousness so that we grow in maturity as Christ followers.

And, So Much More

Along with 2 Timothy 3:16-17, God's Word gives us many other reasons it is so important to us. Our God is huge. He is more than we can handle. He is biggest, strongest, smartest, and most powerful, so much so that there is no way for our finite minds to be able to fully understand His infinite character. It's just too much. But the Bible gives us all that we need to know about the character of God. It tells us who He is and what He is like. It tells us what He did and how He used others. It tells where He is and teaches us His will. We know God because we have His Word. There's no way to write all the verses that show us attributes of God, so I will share some that are most meaningful to me. God is faithful. 2 Timothy 2:13 says, *"If we are faithless, he remains faithful, for he cannot disown himself."* Malachi 3:6 reminds us that God never changes when He says, *"'I the Lord do not change. So, you, the descendants of Jacob, are not destroyed.'"* And, God doesn't need us. John 5:26 tells us that *"... the Father has life in himself..."* But it also tells us that God wants us anyway. In Leviticus 26:12, He lets us know that He wants to be our God and He wants us to be His people.

God's Word is also what lets us know what God does. God loves us so much He sent His son to die in our place (John 3:16). God is faithful to forgive us (1 John 1:9). God protects us (2 Thessalonians 3:3). He fights for us (Deut. 20:4). He prepares us (Ephesians 6:10-18). He will always be with us (Joshua 1:9). He gives us life (John 10:10). He redeems us (Ephesians 1:7). He conquered death and the grave (1 Corinthians 15:54-57). He is coming back for us (John 14:1-4). When you finish reading this chapter, go back and look up these verses for yourself, and even memorize them. I'm so thankful we have the Bible to reveal who God is to us.

Memorizing Scripture just isn't a priority for most Christians today, myself included. So, I'm definitely preaching to myself here. We think we know what it means, so there's really no need to know it word for word. But this simply isn't true. We can look to none other than Jesus to give example to this. When Jesus was led to the wilderness to be tempted, there was only one way He resisted the temptation. It was through the memorization of Scripture. All three times Satan tempted, Jesus came back at him with the Sword of the Spirit, which is the Word of God. Satan told Him to make the stones become bread, to which He replied, *"Man shall not live on bread alone, but on every word that comes from the mouth of God"* (Matthew 4:4). This verse is found in Deuteronomy 8:3, and Jesus had committed it to memory! Satan again tempts Jesus to prove He's God by jumping off a cliff so the angels could rescue Him. See, Jesus wouldn't jump off a cliff just because someone asked Him to jump. Jesus responds with Scripture He had memorized. *"Do not put the Lord your God to the test"* (Matthew 4:7). This verse is found in Deuteronomy 6:16, and, once again, Jesus had memorized it. Satan's last attempt to make Jesus fall into temptation was when he told Jesus he would give Him all kingdoms of the world and all splendor if He would only bow and worship Satan, as if he had some kind of authority. And, because Jesus had memorized Deuteronomy 6:13, He replied, *"Worship the Lord your God, and serve Him only"* (Matthew 4:10).

I whole-heartedly believe Jesus was tempted like us so he could become our *"merciful and faithful high priest"* (Hebrews 2:17). The only way for Jesus to be our substitute sacrifice is if He was tempted like us but found innocent. However, I also believe Jesus was tempted in order to give us the ultimate example of what to use when we are tempted -- God's Word. Our temptation is no surprise to our Lord. He knew we would struggle, and therefore He knew we would need to know the best way to combat Satan. Church girl, there is no better way to fight the devil's schemes than with the only thing that is *"alive and active,"* *"sharper than any double-edged sword,"* *"dividing soul and spirit, joints and marrow,"* and that *"judges the thoughts and attitudes of the heart"* (Hebrews 4:12). It is the Word of God. Learn it. Know it. Memorize it.

When We Don't Know God's Word

Since I'm in a story-telling kind of mood, humor me once again. Once upon a time, there was a man who was a mighty warrior, so mighty, in fact, that his nation asked him to lead their army to defeat their fierce enemy. They even told him that if he commanded the army, he would also be head over all who lived in the nation. So, he made the deal and became commander of the army. First, he tried diplomatic efforts by sending a messenger to talk to the enemy. It didn't work. Nevertheless, this mighty warrior, desperate to win the battle, made a promise to God. He promised that if God would deliver them from their fierce enemy, he would sacrifice whatever came out to meet him first when he returned home as a burnt offering. God delivered them, and the battle was won. When this victorious soldier returned home, he was not met by cattle or his dog. He wasn't met by his donkey or chickens. His daughter, celebrating and dancing, was the first out to meet him. Devastated and in torment, he explained the promise he made in order to win the victory, and, eventually, did to her what he had promised.

Such a sad story, huh? What would you say to this mighty warrior? Would you mourn with him? Would you explain that it really isn't a big deal to go back on his promise? Would you try to rescue the daughter from her perilous fate? We all probably have a thing or two to say to this soldier, but I would tell him one thing. I would tell him to study God's Word and law. I would tell him to commit it to memory. You see, this is a true story. You can read about it in Judges 11. His name was Jephthah. Had he known what the Lord had already said about making a vow, as well as what it said about sacrificing humans, this story would be slightly different. Clearly, Jephthah was not familiar with God's law. In Leviticus 5:4-6 we learn that:

If anyone thoughtlessly takes an oath to do anything, whether good or evil (in any matter one might carelessly swear about) even though they are unaware of it, but then they learn of it and realize their guilt – when anyone becomes aware that they are guilty in any of these matters, they must confess in what way they have sinned. As a penalty for the sin they have committed, they must bring to the Lord a female lamb

or goat from the flock as a sin offering, and the priest
shall make atonement for them for their sin.

I know that's a lot, so let's break it down. These verses are basically saying you shouldn't make a rash vow, but, if you do and you realize you shouldn't have, you can bring a sin offering before the Lord. So, whether this text is taken literally, and he really sacrificed his daughter or whether it is believed that she was given to the Lord with a life of celibacy, which some scholars believe, all could have been avoided had he known and practiced God's Word.

I know this story of Jephthah is serious with serious, life-altering consequences, but we are guilty of the same thing. Believe it or not, neglecting to know and practice God's Word has consequences. The biggest consequence is not knowing Jesus and spending eternity in hell. But there are other consequences as well. If we don't know God's Word, we will resolve conflict the wrong way, resulting in ruined relationships. If we don't know God's Word, we will date someone who doesn't believe in Jesus like we do, resulting in a life-long marriage of struggles that are passed on to our children. Take it from Jephthah. We must know the Word. We must live by the Word. We must hide the Word in our hearts.

My Delight

We've examined so much about God's Word and how it trains us in righteousness by teaching, rebuking and correcting, how it reveals God's character and His will, how it is used to fight temptation, and even how it is devastating when we do not know it. But, there's one more beautiful reason to read the Bible. It is our delight. This took me so long, way too long, to grasp. I grew up memorizing scripture. I come from a family full of preachers and then went on to marry one. I was practically born wearing my Sunday dress, and my life had been inundated with Scripture. But, for whatever reason, it took too long for me to fall in love with it. To delight in it. I'm talking the kind of love where you long for it and dream about it. Where it consumes not just your mind but your heart, soul, emotions, and every fiber of your being. This is the kind of delight the Psalmist talks about, especially in Psalm 119. Y'all, stop reading right now, open up your Bible to this chapter and read it. Soak it up. Pray over it. Ok, so it is the longest Psalm, so you might want to break it up a little. It's probably divided into sections in your Bible, so pray over each one every day for the next two weeks. This is good stuff!

So, what does delight mean anyway? Dictionary.com defines delight as "to have great pleasure" or "take pleasure." It defines pleasure as "enjoyment or satisfaction derived from what is to one's liking; gratification; delight."[12] So, we can assume that delighting in God's Word would mean to have great enjoyment, satisfaction and thankfulness for those sacred words. And, the Psalmist gets it. He mentions delighting in the Word nine different times in chapter 119 alone.

I delight in your decrees; I will not neglect your word.
Ps. 119:16

Your statutes are my delight; they are my counselors.
Ps. 119:24

Direct me in the path of your commands, for there
I find delight.
Ps. 119:35

I will speak of your statutes before kings and will not be
put to shame, for I delight in your commands because I
love them.
Ps. 119:46-47

Their hearts are callous and unfeeling, but I delight
in your law.
Psalm 119:70

Let your compassion come to me that I may live, for your
law is my delight.
Ps. 119:77

If your law had not been my delight, I would have
perished in my affliction.
Ps. 119:92

Trouble and distress have come upon me, but your
commands give me delight.
Ps. 119:143

I long for your salvation, Lord, and your law
gives me delight.
Ps. 119:174

Oh, to be at the place where we delight in Scripture. Where it's the first help we go to in trouble. The place where it's our comfort during the storm. Our strength during our failures. Our best friend when we are lonely. Oh, to be at the place where God's Word is our joy. Our satisfaction. Our enjoyment. Our everything. Lord, let your Word be our closest companion, guiding, friending, lifting, fighting for and encouraging us. Let it be a *"lamp for my feet, a light for on path"* (Ps. 119:105). Let it be our pleasure. Lord, let it be our delight. And, it's ok to pray for this. Ask for the desire to delight in the Word. Ask and ask again for a longing to know and love Scripture. It's a beautiful place to be.

The End -- And the Beginning

This really is a big deal. Reading, living and loving Scripture really is a big deal, and it will change your life completely. It's really hard to sum up everything that the Bible means to us and all it accomplishes, but this quote from an anonymous writer gives us a beautiful picture of the value of God's Word.

The Bible does not contain the Word of God, it is the Word of God and it does contain: The Mind of God, the state of man, the way of salvation, the doom of sinners, and the happiness of believers! Its doctrine is holy, its precepts are binding, its histories are true and its decisions are immutable! Read it to be wise, believe it to be saved and practice it to be holy! It contains light to direct you, food to support you, and comfort to cheer you! It is the traveler's map, the pilgrim's staff, the pilot's compass, the soldier's sword and the Christian's charter! Here heaven is opened, and the gates of hell disclosed! Christ is its grand subject, our good its design and the glory of God its end! It should fill the memory, rule the heart, and guide the feet! Read it slowly, frequently, and prayerfully! It is a mine of wealth, health to the soul, and a river of pleasure! It is given to you here in this life, will be opened at the judgment, and is established forever! It involves the highest responsibility, will reward the greatest labor, and condemn all who trifle with its contents![13]

Fall in love with God's Word,

Holly

Make it Stick, Church Girl

1. What is the hardest part of God's Word to believe as absolute truth? Why?

2. Read Psalm 119:160. What promises does this verse give?

3. Read Hebrews 4:12. What do you think it means that the Word of God is "living?"

4. God's Word is just as relevant today as it was when it was written because it is living. It is able to carry out activities as the Living God would because it is God. The very words we read are Jesus Himself. Check out John 1:14!

5. Name a few ways that Scripture was able to teach, rebuke, or correct you recently.

6. Write a prayer, asking the Lord to give you a longing and delight for His Word.

Dear Church Girl, God's Word is Truth, No Matter Your Opinions

Let's be honest. It's really easy to offend people these days. That statement alone probably offended someone. My apologies. But doesn't it seem we are living in a world that is so politically driven that everything is open to opinion? We have opinions about many different things. We debate over whether Coca Cola or Pepsi tastes better or whether it should be 68 degrees or 72 degrees in our homes. We differ on whether we should lower taxes to promote job growth or increase taxes to fund more government. We disagree on animal rights issues and even human rights issues. Welcome to America, where we even disagree about whether the toilet paper should roll in or out, for crying out loud. Nevertheless, everyone has an opinion about something.

Some of us are loud with our opinions, holding our picket signs and shouting chants, and plastering it on social media to be sure we spark a debate. Then there are those of us who have opinions but keep them quiet, avoiding the conversation and happily skipping through a life without any controversy. And, some of us are just in between the two extremes. With all this being said, there is a right and wrong way to have an opinion, regardless of what society teaches or what you've seen on the news. We are going to take a look at not only what opinions we have but also how we are expressing and living out those opinions.

Our Rights

We live in America, the Land of the Free and the Home of the Brave. As citizens of this great nation, we have rights. We have the right to freedom, the right to choose who we will worship and where, the right to speak and vote, the right to be silent and the right to an impartial jury, just to name a few. I read an article the other day about a man who is actually suing his parents for giving birth to him because he never gave them permission to do so. I can't make this stuff up. But he has a right to try to sue his parents. We all have this right and many more. But only as citizens of the United States.

If we have surrendered our lives to Jesus, we have given up our rights, American citizens or not. We no longer have the right to worship something else. We no longer have the right to speak just anything we want. We do not have the right to be silent or the right to an impartial jury. You see, when we choose to follow Jesus, we relinquished all of our rights over to Him and what He wants. Ephesians 2:19 tells us:

Consequently, you are no longer foreigners and aliens, but fellow citizens with God's people and members of God's household....

Therefore, we seek to worship only Him always and to only speak words that would please Him. Anything less than this is an offense. This is what we call sin. And here's where the right to impartial jury is given up. God is holy and righteous; therefore, He will give our verdict, and you better believe His is partial. He loves us so stinkin' much that He came to earth to die for us and pay the penalty for abusing what freedoms we thought we should have. So, what does this have to do with our opinions? If we are Christ followers and our opinion does not line up with God's truth, we have absolutely no right to that opinion. We relinquished that right when we gave our lives to Christ. Remember, we are not our own, and God's Word is true no matter what our opinions are. No matter what the President's opinions are. No matter what the Pope's opinions are. No matter what your professor's opinions are. No matter what your pastor's opinions are. And certainly, no matter what CNN, Fox News, or MSNBC's opinions are. God's Word is the absolute truth; therefore, we relinquish our "opinions" at the feet of our Savior. Jesus said:

If you hold to my teaching, you are really my disciples.
Then you will know the truth, and the truth will
set you free.
John 8:31-32

Apart from truth, there is no salvation, no freedom, no rights but only empty opinions that lie to us and hold us captive.

Our Reasoning

We establish our opinions on many things. We like Coca Cola better than Pepsi because it tastes better. We chose Nike over Adidas because the shoes feel better. Sometimes we base our opinions on what is convenient for us or what will make us more money or what will cause us to achieve this goal or that goal. Sometimes, we make our choices seem right, and we may even allow society to form our opinions for us.

Frequently, we like to jump on the band wagon of opinions about especially controversial topics because of certain injustices happening around the world. This can be healthy, and we are called to stand up for the weak. Proverbs 31:8-9 says:

Speak up for those who cannot speak for themselves, for
the rights of all who are destitute. Speak up and judge
fairly; defend the rights of the poor and needy.

The problem lies when we begin to look for what really isn't there. Recently the United States Women's soccer team had the privilege to play in the final game of the World Cup. After winning the last World Cup in 2015, soccer fans across the nation were ecstatic that they would be playing in the second final game in a row! What should have been a time of large celebration and excitement was quickly overshadowed by controversy. It just so happened that the U.S. Men's team was playing the final game of the Gold Cup on the same day. To beat it all, the 2019 Copa America Final was also this same day. Three huge American soccer events on the same day. Poor scheduling? Absolutely. Intentionally trying to sabotage women's soccer? Most likely not. But that's what it turned into. Many insisted that this poor planning that had scheduled two men's finals on the same day as the women's World Cup final was an intentional plot against women. Fighting for injustices that aren't really there is making less of the real injustices and does no one any favors. It's counterproductive. If we are going to be upset about women's soccer, let's stand up for the fact that women aren't getting paid near as much as men when they are the ones actually bringing home the titles. I know, I digress. But looking for petty things to plaster on our picket signs takes the focus from the real injustices around the world, whether concerning women, race, or government.

Our society has covered absolute truth with opinions. But when we listen to society or follow our own hearts, the truth of God's Word becomes blurry. In John 8, Jesus goes on to ask:

Why is my language not clear to you? Because you are unable to hear what I say. You belong to your father, the devil, and you want to carry out your father's desires. He was a murderer from the beginning, not holding to the truth, for there is no truth in him. When he lies, he speaks his native language, for he is a liar and the father of lies.
John 8:43-44

Society has been deceived by the father of all lies. We must test everything against God's Word. Everything we hear from YouTube, the news, music, movies, entertainment, celebrities, churches, pastors, teachers, and even family -- absolutely everything -- should be put to the test. Oh, how blessed we are to have the Truth! Use it. The truth of God's Word should be the foundation for what opinions we form, because God's Word is true, no matter our opinions.

What's the Big Deal, Anyway?

So, why does this matter? I'm so glad you asked! Remember, Paul tells us that:

All scripture is God-breathed and is useful for teaching, rebuking, correcting and training in righteousness, so that the servant of God may be thoroughly equipped for every good work.
2 Timothy 3:16-17

We must test every opinion against the Truth so that we are equipped, so that we are ready for everything God has for us. How are we to point others to the Savior if we are living a lie? How are others going to trust Jesus if we don't even trust Him enough to submit to His truth? For instance, if our opinion is that homosexuality is an acceptable alternative lifestyle, then we are fully saying that there is no truth to the part of God's Word that tells us it is sin. If we believe that because it's the 21st century it's totally acceptable to live with our partner before marriage, we are saying that scripture is wrong in telling us not to have premarital sex. We are calling God a liar, because if it's not truth, it's obviously a lie. Sometimes our lifestyles and opinions scream that God's Word is not true, and we think that it's okay to believe in Jesus and not believe everything the Bible says. But, guess what? Jesus is the Word. The Bible tells us that:

In the beginning was the Word, and the Word was with God and the Word was God.... And the Word became flesh and made his dwelling among us.
John 1:1,14

If you live a life that says God's Word is not completely true, then you live a life that says Jesus is not completely true. And if Jesus is not completely true, there is no rescue for us. There is no Way to God. There is no Life.

This is so necessary for us to grasp. People are dying and going to hell. I know it's not a pretty image and certainly not a topic most people want to discuss, but it is truth. How we live matters because there are lost people watching us. The opinions about which we are so outspoken matter because there are unbelievers looking for Truth, and we've got the answers. But are we to say, "Follow Jesus! He is the only Way. Only, don't listen to that one thing He said in the Bible, but everything else is pretty much great!"? Call me crazy, but I believe most lost people would tip their hats and say, "Not for me!" The "opinions" we foster, especially publicly, can speak lies or truth. Sometimes, we disagree with what God's Word says or claim we don't understand what it says in order to not hurt feelings. We lie about scripture or hide scripture in the name of "loving our neighbor." Absence of Truth = Eternity in Hell. If we love people straight to hell, then all our loving we did here on earth did not mean anything at all. It was all in vain.

Some things won't be so cut and dry. Some things will take lots of praying and searching. And that's okay. But never take a stand for or against something until you are certain it aligns with the Scripture, because the moment your opinion doesn't align with God's truth, it is no longer an opinion but a lie.

Sharing Our Opinions

Hopefully by now you have realized that as a Christ-follower our opinions should always promote the truth of Jesus and His Word. But, how do we publicly and effectively share these opinions, or even truths, with others. This is where so many believers struggle. I have been extremely outspoken most of my life, and it took a long while for me to learn the art of holding strong opinions in a way that honors Christ. So, how do we do it?

In Love. In some of Paul's final words to the first letter he sent the church in Corinth, he urges:

Be on your guard; stand firm in the faith; be courageous; be strong. Do everything in love.
1 Corinthians 16:13-14

Paul had just written an entire letter (1 Corinthians) to this church teaching them about Christian conduct. He speaks to the church about developing a holy character, touching on topics such as divisions, immaturity, jealousy, lawsuits, sexual immorality, and using our spiritual gifts, just to name a few. He knew that sending this church out to reach their community for Jesus meant they were going to be confronted with a society who could care less about the risen Savior. He knew it would be difficult for them to stand up for truth, so he gives them words such as "be on guard" and "stand firm" and "be courageous" to encourage them. But he ends the phrase with "Do everything in love." So, what does it mean to do everything in love? Well, it just so happens that Paul addressed this very topic earlier in this letter.

Love is patient, love is kind. It does not envy, it does not boast, it is not proud. It does not dishonor others, it is not self-seeking, it is not easily angered, it keeps no record of wrongs. Love does not delight in evil but rejoices with the truth. It always protects, always trusts, always hopes, always perseveres.
I Corinthians 13:4-7

Paul is fairly detailed when it comes to defining love. When we are taking a stand for truth, we must be sure we deliver the message with patience, not expecting unbelievers to fully understand our point of view. We must also do it with kindness, only speaking words that would build up; therefore, we should never engage in behavior such as name-calling or profanity. We should share truth without boasting. Remember, it's not about us, it's about Jesus. It's hard to debate without being easily angered, but that's exactly what we are also called to do. We have to remember that love is not only an action but also a reaction; therefore, when others are impatient, unkind, boastful, and dishonoring, we should respond in love. And, church girls, if we can't share our opinions in love, we need to keep them to ourselves.

With the right motives. Jesus knows our intentions. He knows if we are sharing our opinions to stir up trouble or to get a negative reaction from someone. He knows if we are giving it to start a fight or because we are angry at someone, and He knows if we are doing it out of revenge. It's counterproductive to share truth while having a lying heart. Always be sure you are sharing truth in love and for the right reasons. One right reason might be to reach someone for Christ. Another right reason may be to stand up for injustices, such as holding signs or praying outside an abortion clinic. Some right motives might be to shed light on sin and sharing with your best friend the reason she should not move in with her boyfriend. But whatever the right reason, always, always do it with a pure motive and much love.

Is it worth it? Let's face it, some opinions are just not worth sharing. It's easy to let disputes that matter little make a major negative impact on our relationships with others. 2 Timothy 2:23-24 says:

> *Don't have anything to do with foolish and stupid arguments, because you know they produce quarrels. And the Lord's servant must not be quarrelsome but must be kind to everyone, able to teach, not resentful.*

To clear up any confusion, we are the Lord's servant Paul mentions here; we are the Christ-follower who should refrain from situations and conversations that could lead to stupid arguments about things that don't matter much. Be sure that whatever opinion you decide to publicly give is well worth the relationship that it may cost you to give it.

What They Want You to Believe

Everyone seems to be pushing an agenda these days. Our current society wants you to believe certain ways in order to advance what is on their agendas, especially the ones who have been given the biggest platform, whether through media or fame. With topics such as global warming, being eco-friendly, following your heart, women's rights, co-existing, or prosperity-driven ambitions on the rise, we have got to take what is being thrown at us with a grain of salt. We must stack it against God's Word. Do you know why? Because we have an agenda, too. Or, at least we should. We have a God-given agenda. An agenda that has the potential to change the world. What is it? God's Word gives us our full agenda. He tells us to *"offer your bodies as living sacrifices, holy and pleasing to God"* (Romans 12:1), to *"Let your light shine before others, that they may see your good deeds and glorify your Father in heaven"* (Matthew 5:16), and *"Therefore go and make disciples of all nations"* (Matthew 28:19). And these are just a few of the details of our agenda. The Bible gives us many more. The point is, anything and everything that our society tries to push on us, we must make sure it lines up with Scripture. If society is telling us to do whatever feels right and follow our heart but the Bible tells us that our *"heart is deceitful above all things,"* (Jeremiah 17:9) obviously, we should not trust our feelings or our heart no matter what celebrities, politicians, or Cinderella herself may say. And not every agenda in our current culture today is at odds with scripture. There's a push to prioritize caring for our environment and earth, and the Bible tells us to *"fill the earth and subdue it"* (Genesis 1:28) and to *"not pollute the land where you are"* nor *"defile the land where you live"* (Numbers 35:33-34). So, therefore, we should be making every effort we can to take care of the land in which we live. On the other hand, society would have you to believe that true success and fulfillment in life come from money or material things. God's Word tells us that:

Godliness with contentment is great gain. For we brought nothing into the world, and we can take nothing out of it...the love of money is the root of all kinds of evil
1 Timothy 6:6-7,10

Because of these verses, we should look for contentment in Jesus, not all the "stuff" we have.

Learn early on to test everything you hear from society, media, entertainment, famous people, humanitarians, or even the church to see if it agrees with what God has told you. We can't let others form our views and opinions for us but instead must *"...test them all; hold on to what is good"* (1 Thessalonians 5:21). And, let's be okay swimming upstream when everyone else is swimming downstream because we know we are pleasing the One who redeemed us and gave His life for us.

How Do We Do This?

When we were young, our parents set out rules, guidelines, and disciplines for us. They set up boundaries they felt sure would keep us safe and taught us to live by them. They also helped shape how we view the world and interpret its philosophies. In other words, if your parents believe that we should build a border wall, that recycling isn't necessary, or that KJV is the only version of the Bible you should read, chances are that has affected the opinions you have about those topics. If you grew up in a family who believes women should have the right to choose, who drank real wine at communion, or who wore jeans to church on Sunday, chances are these have affected your views about such. Romans 12:1-2 says:

Therefore, I urge you brothers and sisters, in view of God's mercy to offer your bodies as a living sacrifice, holy and pleasing to God – this is your true and proper worship. Do not conform to the pattern of this world, but be transformed by the renewing of your mind. Then you will be able to test and approve what God's will is – his good, pleasing and perfect will.

Because God spared us from the eternal death we deserve, we are to be completely set apart for His use. To do this we must refrain from living like the world and instead continually change our way of thinking to agree with God's word. Then we will be able to test what matches His will and what doesn't, and His will is always perfect. If you are struggling to find clarity when issues aren't so clear, I recommend you read *Chasing Elephants: Wrestling with the Gray Areas of Life* by Brent Crowe, Ph.D. This brilliant book gives you a practical tool to use when things aren't so cut and dry. It really should be the next book you pick up and read.

Church girls, do not be afraid to take what you've learned your whole life and make sure it actually does match the will of God. Whether it's from your parents, family, pastor, teachers, or friends, all should be put to the test before you form an opinion. Don't be like me. I waited way too long to start putting things to the test. Remember, the moment our opinion doesn't align with God's truth, it is no longer an opinion but a lie.

God's Word is truth,

Holly

Make it Stick, Church Girl

1. Are there opinions you have that are purely based on how you were raised or what cultural views are trending? List some below.

2. Below are some "hot topic" issues in which you have most likely already formed an opinion. Write what you believe or how you feel about each next to the issue. Then, write what God's Word says about each issue, listing where you found it in the Bible.

Pro-life/Pro-choice
  My Opinion:

  God's Word:

Government Welfare
  My Opinion:

  God's Word:

Tithing
My Opinion:

God's Word:

Church Attendance
My Opinion:

God's Word:

Social Drinking
My Opinion:

God's Word:

Homosexuality
My Opinion:

God's Word:

3. What opinions have you shared in the past that have hindered your influence to share the Gospel with someone?

4. Are there any truths you have neglected to share in the name of "loving your neighbor?" List them below.

Dear Church Girl, Pray First, Then Ask Siri

My intention for this chapter is to drive home how important it is to pray before you look elsewhere for answers like Siri, Alexa, your bestie, or your dog. It occurred to me, however, that learning what prayer is and how to do it was something I learned early in my adult life. Oh, how I wish I would have really grasped this sooner. This girl who was in church multiple times a week, attended every camp or revival, sang in worship, and knew Jesus personally really did not get just how important prayer is. I'm so glad I know now but can't help thinking there are church girls reading this who haven't yet realized not only the significance of a healthy prayer life but also how to really pray in general.

We hear certain prayers growing up in church. They may start something like, "Dear Heavenly Father, thank you for this day." And they may end with "In Your Precious Name we pray, Amen." And these prayers may have everything in between these two phrases such as give us a good day, thank you for this food, and be with all the sick. Sound familiar? Our prayers can become monotone, meaningless sets of phrases put together without even thinking about it. Most of us could almost pray subconsciously. Talking to the Lord is not supposed to be this way. He wants so much more out of our relationship with Him. So, let's take a few minutes to really dive into how we should pray.

What's Prayer Got to Do with It?

I was 15 years old when terrorists attacked the World Trade Center on 9/11. I remember watching the live coverage from my English class. We were devastated. We were scared. We were confused. One thing I'll never forget is how everyone seemed to come together to pray for our nation. There were signs asking people to pray, memorial services with prayer, and leaders of NYC and our country asking our entire nation to pray. People who I was certain could not possibly be Christians were suddenly praying. What else was there to do in such a helpless situation but turn to God. And for a lot of people, many Christians included, this is the only time prayer becomes important. Many only pray when something is wrong, like someone is sick or someone lost their job or someone got their feelings hurt. These are the times when we cry out to God. While this is good and is what we are supposed to do when devastation occurs, prayer is about so much more. Prayer is important, even when everything seems to be going right. Knowing the value of praying to the Sustainer of Life may be what compels us to pray more. Let's take a look at some reasons why we should pray.

Prayer deepens our relationship with Jesus. James tells us to "come near to God and he will come near to you" (James 4:8). Often when we feel God is distant, we have to remember that He never moves; we do. Are we talking to Him enough to actually be close to Him? Going to church, celebrating Christian holidays, making good choices, going to youth camp, and volunteering for missions can only do so much for our personal relationship with Jesus. We must talk to Him, and we must listen to Him. Psalm 145:18 tells us that the "Lord is near to all who call on Him, to all who call on Him in truth." God is continually chasing after us, wanting a deeper relationship, but we are the ones to blame for a distant relationship because we are not talking to Him. And, did you know that we are supposed to enjoy the Lord and delight in Him? We see this all throughout the Bible. Isaiah 61:10 says,

I will delight greatly in the Lord; my soul rejoices in my God. For he has clothed me with garments of salvation.

And according to Psalm 16:11, we can experience this enjoyment when we are in His presence.

You make known to me the path of life, you will fill me with joy in your presence, with eternal pleasures at your right hand.

C.S. Lewis said, "Prayer in the sense of petition, asking for things, is a small part of it, confession and penitence are its threshold, adoration its sanctuary, the presence and vision and enjoyment of God its bread and wine."[14]

Prayer alleviates anxiety. Look, ya'll be stressin'. It used to be that the parents with full time careers and families were the ones who were stressed, but things sure have changed. I never remember really being stressed until I was married with a family, but I have seen a dramatic increase in the stress level of young women in the past several years. In a survey conducted by the American Psychological Association, teens report their stress level to be 5.8 out of 10 during the school year with 31% admitting their stress levels have increased over the past year.[15] Church girls, you all are stressed out. Guess what? Prayer alleviates stress. No joke, it really does. Not only do I know this from personal experiences in my own very stressful, often chaotic life, but scripture tells us too. Philippians 4:6-7 commands us:

Do not be anxious about anything, but in every situation, by prayer and petition, with thanksgiving, present your requests to God. And the peace of God, which transcends all understanding, will guard your hearts and your minds in Christ Jesus.

Ya'll, I can think of no better word to describe the opposite of anxiety than peace. And, that's exactly what we get when we present our requests to God.

Prayer helps us to avoid temptation. This is a big one for me, probably you too. By the time you get to my age, you are in full realization of just how messed up you really are. And, boy, am I messed up. After years of knowing Jesus, loving Jesus, growing closer to Jesus, how is it that I still struggle so much with certain temptations? Ya feel me? I sure hope I'm not the only one. When Jesus went up to the Mount of Olives to pray before His death, He told His disciples to *"pray that you will not fall into temptation"* before He left for His personal prayer time alone with God (Luke 22:40). But they didn't pray. Instead, the disciples fell asleep. The soldiers came, Judas betrayed Jesus, and Peter lost his cool and cut off a soldier's ear, and the rest of the disciples ran away. They all gave into temptation. I can't help but think of so many instances where I said something rude, neglected a responsibility, yelled at my kids, lost my temper and much, much worse. Would the outcome have been different had I prayed about it? Would my reactions have been different had I retreated and prayed like Jesus? Probably. Taking time to stop and ask Jesus to help you stay away from temptation and to be able to stand firm against it may be just what is needed to overcome it.

Prayer gives us an opportunity to ask for forgiveness. We sin. Most of us daily. We try. We fail. We sin again. Most of us daily. We are like a broken record. Ladies, there should be a time every single day when we are not only asking Jesus to forgive us for all of our sins but also to reveal our sin to us. Because of our flesh, we often don't always realize when we are dishonoring God. As David shows us, asking God to *"create in me a pure heart"* and *"renew a stead-fast spirit within me"* will lead to restoring the *"joy of our salvation"* which will sustain us (Psalm 51:10-12). Jesus paid the penalty and our sins are forgiven once and for all. Because of this we should be continually asking Jesus to show us the sin in our life, so that we can love Him better.

Prayer gives us answers. And, church girls, we are in desperate need of answers. When we are faced with choices to make, prayer should always be the first route we take on the road to deciding. James tells us that *"if any of you lacks wisdom, you should ask God, who gives generously to all without finding fault, and it will be given to you"* (James 1:5). I don't know about you, but I sure am lacking wisdom on most days. Pray for answers. Pray for wisdom.

Prayer allows us to hear from God. I love to talk to God, and sometimes I forget that God wants to talk to me, too. He does this several ways, with the usual way being through His Word. Pray as you read. Pray for God to reveal His Word, His promises, His desires and Himself to you. This is ultimately how we will get the answers He wants to give us.

When Do We Pray?

Now that we've discussed a little bit about why prayer is so important, let's talk about when we should be praying. There's a simple answer to this question: All. The. Time. 1 Thessalonians 5:17 tells us to *"pray continually."* Other versions say *"without ceasing."* In other words, talking to

Jesus should be so common and happen so often that we are in a continual conversation with Him. I'm not there yet, but that's exactly where I want to be. There are, however, some specific times where praying to the Lord is warranted.

I believe we should be praying every morning. It should become part of our routine. We live in a world where distractions are normal and life is crazy. Taking time out each morning reminds us of who and what is most important. It reminds us to live out our day intentionally. And, it allows us to thank and praise our Creator, Sustainer, and Savior. Psalm 5:3 says:

In the morning, Lord, you hear my voice; in the morning I lay my requests before you and wait expectantly.

Yes, we can do this any time, but talking to Jesus in the morning is the best way to start our day and gets us excited about what He is going to do! We pray in the morning and wait expectantly for God to move. And, as we pray, we should watch for His answer. Colossians 4:2 says, *"Devote yourselves to prayer, being watchful and thankful."* With thankful hearts we watch – expectantly - for the Lord to answer our prayer.

Several times in Scripture we read about Jesus retreating from everyone else to talk to the Father. Luke tells us that *"Jesus often withdrew to lonely places and prayed"* (Luke 5:16). Praying in church is great, but it can't replace our alone time with Jesus. We must retreat. We must withdraw from people, our phones, society, social media, entertainment, and everything else to be alone with our Savior. This will draw us closer to Him and make it easier to hear His voice and sense His presence. We need to do this often, just as Jesus did. This can be difficult, especially in society where corporate prayer is the thing to do for the cultural Christian. We pray together before football games, together at church, together before we eat dinner, and we even make bedtime prayer a family affair. By the end of the day, we've already prayed three times and think we are in good shape! While it's not a bad thing to pray together, these prayers are not what deepens and strengthens our relationship with Jesus. Instead it's our time spent alone with Him.

To completely answer the question of when we need to pray, we can also refer to the previous section about why we should be praying. We are to pray when we want to grow closer to Him, when we need forgiveness, when we are anxious, when we have requests or need to make decisions, when we are struggling with temptation, when we just watched him do something grand, and when we want to hear from Him. In other words, we should talk to the Lord all the time.

We Learn From the Best

While tucking my 8-year old daughter in bed one night, she began to pray. "Jesus, give Papaw Jim's leg the authority to walk again [he's an amputee] and help me not to yell at the doctor who tries to give me a shot [flu vaccine], and help the mac-n-cheese I had for dinner not to make me constipated [no explanation here]." While we can learn to be honest and while we can learn that God cares about all of our needs by listening to Annabeth's prayer, it is not exactly the best example of how to pray. The greatest example we have of prayer is from Jesus Himself.

This, then, is how you should pray: "Our Father in Heaven, hallowed by your name, your kingdom come, your will be done, on earth as it is in heaven. Give us today our daily bread. And forgive us our debts, as we also have forgiven our debtors. And lead us not into temptation but deliver us from the evil one."
Matthew 6:9-13

There are several points to draw from this example of prayer Jesus gives us. He begins this prayer with adoration and praise. He acknowledges who God is and that He is holy. He tells God He is the best, the greatest, the One above all else. We should be telling the Lord what we think of Him and how much we love Him and why! This is part of our worship and gives us the opportunity to adore the One who broke our chains of sin and death. Recognizing who God is and what He has done for us before we bring our requests to Him helps us to pray with faith that He holds everything in His hands. I mean, think about it. The creator of the universe wants to talk with us. That's incredible and reason enough to begin our prayer with adoration and praise.

Jesus then asks for the Lord's will to be done. This is hard. He also prayed something similar in the Garden of Gethsemane before His death. He prayed, *"My Father, if it is not possible for this cup to be taken away unless I drink it, may your will be done"* (Matthew 26:42). Knowing that it would bring Him a cruel death He did not deserve, Jesus still prayed for God's will to be done. Often when we pray, we are asking for things to happen like a sick person to be healed, a good grade on a test we've studied so hard for, or that job we've always wanted. But what if God's will is different than what we want? Telling God that you want His will to be done is like telling Him that we know His ways are higher than our ways (Isaiah 55:9). This is not easy to do but necessary for full surrender to Jesus and what He wants for our lives.

When my son used to get scared at night, he always asked me to pray. Pray that the storm goes away or pray that bad guys won't break in or pray that no one will die. And I prayed for those things, but I also prayed that we would put all of our trust in the Lord. I prayed that if what God chooses isn't what we want, that we would trust in His plan and know that He will never leave us. Jaxon wasn't always happy with this. He wanted all his problems, worries, and storms taken away, but we know that's just not life. We've got to learn to fully surrender to the Lord's will and trust Him with the results.

Next, He asks God to give us our daily bread. We can think of this part of the prayer as presenting our requests. We have to be careful here, however, God is not a genie. He doesn't grant us wishes based on our fleshly desires. Sometimes our prayers become a long to-do list for God, a long list much like what we used to write for Santa when we were little. Yes, we should be praying for the sick to be healed, our future to be successful, our family to be safe, and such. But we should be examining our desires on a regular basis. Our deepest desire should be to want what God wants. In other words, we should pray that His desires become our desires. I think we would see a drastic change in the long list of requests we give Jesus. Jesus already knows what we need, but we don't. We don't have a clue. We like to think we do, but we don't. We have to trust that God's desires are good enough for us and exactly all that we need.

The next part of this example prayer is tough also. Matthew 6:12 says, *"And forgive us our debts, as we also have forgiven our debtors."* Look at the specific order this is in. We can't approach the Lord for forgiveness if we have not already forgiven those who have wronged us. It is probably already assumed that the people He is preaching to on this Sermon on the Mount already knows to forgive others before asking God to forgive because Jesus has already addressed it in the same sermon. In Matthew 5:23-24 Jesus says:

If you are offering your gift at the altar and there remember that your brother or sister has something against you, leave your gift there in front of the altar. First go and be reconciled to them; then come and offer your gift.

Then He also reiterates it again in verses 14-15 in chapter six, *"For if you forgive other people when they sin against you, your Heavenly Father will also forgive you."* Not forgiving others will hinder our relationship with Christ. We'll talk more about this later. We need to pray for forgiveness -- after we forgive others.

The last part of this example prayer refers to temptation, which we've already talked about in this chapter. But it's important enough to talk about again. First of all, let me clear up a common misconception. God does not tempt us to sin. Ever. James 1:13 says, *"When tempted, no one* should say, 'God is tempting me.' For God cannot be tempted by evil, nor does he tempt anyone." So, there's that. Being tempted is not God's fault. It's a product of our broken world. As I mentioned before, Jesus gave clear instructions to the disciples to pray so they would not fall into temptation. They were catchin' z's instead of talking to God, which ended with Peter's denial, Jesus' best friends bailing on Him, and an ear lying on the ground. It's no wonder Jesus addresses this in His model prayer for us. He knows prayer is necessary to combat temptation.

How Not to Pray

Just as Jesus gave us an example of how we should pray to the Father, He also tells us how not to pray. And, he actually addresses this just before showing them how to pray. Matthew 6:5-8 says:

And when you pray, do not be like the hypocrites, for they love to pray standing in the synagogues and on the street corners to be seen by others. Truly I tell you, they have received their reward in full. But when you pray, go into your room, close the door and pray to your Father, who is unseen. Then your Father, who sees what is done in secret, will reward you. And when you pray, do not keep on babbling like pagans, for they think they will be heard because of their many words. Do not be like them, for your Father knows what you need before you ask him.

The main point to be made here is we should never pray to show off, whether we are trying to show off to those around us or to God, Himself. This is a heart issue. Remember the subconscious, meaningless prayers we talked about earlier? Talking to Jesus doesn't have to be wordy or flowery or poetic. It's an intimate conversation between you and God. And our heart has everything to do with it. Our intentions or motives for praying publicly should never be so that we are seen or heard by others. In Luke 18:9-14, Jesus tells a parable of two different men who went to the temple to pray. The first one was a Pharisee who said, *"God, I thank you that I'm not like other people – robbers, evildoers, adulterers – or even like this tax collector. I fast twice a week and give a tenth of all I get."* Well, good for you, Mr. Pharisee, but God knows your heart, bro. Meanwhile, the tax collector couldn't even look toward heaven when he said, "God have mercy on me, a sinner." Because of his humbleness, Jesus said he "went home justified before God." When we pray with haughty spirits whether in private or public, God does not credit it as righteousness, and we do not leave His throne justified.

What if I Can't Pray?

We've all probably been there at some point, and, if we haven't yet, we are sure to experience it in the future. Sometimes, we just can't pray. Maybe it's because the hurt is too deep or the guilt too great. Maybe it's because we are too angry. Maybe our loss is too much for us to put into words. There was a time in my very young adult life when I really struggled with anxiety. Sometimes, I worked myself up so much that I was almost over the edge. When I got to this point, I would just freeze. I know you've heard of "flight or fight," meaning upon a stressful or scary situation, we tend to either take flight and run or stay and fight it out. But, in my case, I would just freeze. I could not talk about it, let alone actually do something about it. I would just freeze and cry, of course, but my point is that I could not pray. I did not have the words. I'm sure this sounds familiar to a few of you. Do you know what the good news is? We have one who intercedes for us. Romans 8:26 tells us that the *"Spirit helps us in our weakness"* and that *"...we do not know what we ought to pray for, but the Spirit himself intercedes for us through wordless groans."* It's good to have a few prayer warriors who will sincerely pray for us when we reach this point. But know that even if we feel we are fighting all alone, the Holy Spirit is on our side, praying on our behalf. What an encouragement!

This Just All Feels Weird

When talking to God is not part of our every day, it can feel awkward trying to strike up a conversation with Him. Let me explain. We moved to a small town when my son, Jaxon, was ten months old. We lived there for over six years before moving to another city the summer after Jaxon's first grade year. He had made many friends, some of whom he still misses. Jaxon is almost finished with his fifth-grade year, and we have lived in our new city for almost four years. The other day one of his friends from this small town wanted to video chat with him. He had not spoken with this friend since we moved away. I told him that she would be calling, and he immediately was stressin'. "Mom, I don't remember her that well. What do I say? What do we talk about? It feels kinda weird," Jaxon panicked. I gave him a few ideas to talk about and questions to ask. Their conversation started awkward but ended with smiles and plenty of laughs. Not talking to God makes us distant from Him, and when we are distant from Him, it feels awkward when we try to talk to Him. It's not religion, it's a relationship. We will not have healthy relationships with anyone if there's little communication. It's no different with Jesus. Our relationship with Him will take communication -- a lot of communication. And continual communication will develop into meaningful, intimate conversations with Jesus. So, even if at first it feels awkward or weird, keep praying, and I promise it will eventually become comfortable conversations with your very Best Friend.

Replacing Prayer

I am the world's worst at trying to find answers and researching for solutions all on my own. When there is a problem, I want it fixed, and soon. I realize this is something that goes all the way back to middle school. In 7th grade, I attended New Hope Christian School, a little school in Corryton, Tennessee. Although small, the work was hard and prepared me so well for high school and college. I literally remember being assigned my first research project. I don't remember which book I did the research report on first, but I remember how much fun I had. I remember going to the big public library to search for information about the author and visiting the periodicals to see what others had said about the book. For those of you who don't know what a library is, it's a place with real, actual books that people have written and articles that people have written about books that other people have written. Now we have the internet and all this information is at our fingertips, but back in 1998, you had to actually visit the library to do all of this, and I loved every minute of it. There was something so satisfying about being able to find information and answers out on my own.

And, I will ask questions until I understand and have it figured out. My high school pre-calculus teacher could attest to that. I drove that man crazy with all my questions about domains and dependent variables and independent variables. I could tell you that Delta was the fourth letter of the Greek alphabet, but what in the world was it doing in my math lesson. And then came motherhood. How else was I supposed to know how to take care of a baby if I didn't research and Google about it. It's not like they come with a manual. After motherhood came nursing school. Yes, I realize that's a little backward, and school is supposed to come before babies. But God had other plans. I had to research a lot in nursing school because most of nursing school is trying to figure out the best answer among four correct answers. A lot of my research was really just me trying to self-diagnose, however, because I was so sure I had a few of the 3,486 diseases I was studying.

Needless to say, this is something I struggle with. Searching for answers on our own is not a bad thing in itself, but it became a very unhealthy habit for me because I was only relying on myself and not on my Lord. Stay with me. Every decision we make requires an initial thought on how we are going to choose to take care of it. My initial thought for most of my decisions is "What can I do about it?" And if I don't have a good answer, I do the only logical thing and ask Siri. My family has had so much fun with Siri. Her answers to the questions we ask are nothing short of hysterical. You can ask Siri if aliens exist, and she will reply, "Wait! What's that behind you?" You can ask her if she wants kids, and she says, "I have everything I need in the cloud." Ask her a question about the future like when you will get married, and she will answer, "You can't hurry love. No, you just have to wait." But let's face it. Even Siri doesn't have all the answers. Alexa doesn't have all the answers. Google doesn't have all the answers. YouTube doesn't have all the answers. Our best friends don't have all the answers. Neither do our dogs. We have got to start going to the Lord first. Sure, God gave us a brain, and He expects us to use it. And, that's exactly why we should be praying for clarity, praying for understanding, praying for discernment.

I Got Ninety-Nine Problems

I had three boyfriends in high school other than the one I married, and I never once prayed if I should say "yes" to being their girlfriend. I never asked God if I should continue in relationships. I just assumed that was something I could handle. This resulted in wasting my Freshmen through Sophomore years on three boys I had no business dating.

There were other things I never really prayed much about either. I never prayed about what to wear or what activities I should be involved in or what to eat. I didn't really pray about where to attend college or what I should do with the rest of my life until I became an adult in the real world. And, y'all, that was way too late. Don't get me wrong, I was still going to church, praying a lot, loving Jesus and all that good stuff, but I did not really seek after God's guidance for most of my decisions. It may seem that some of these are small and not that important, but, the decisions and problems get bigger. Your problems might seem so trivial right now. Maybe you are trying to decide which sport to play, which clothes you should wear, what friends to hang out with, or which elective class to take. Starting a habit of praying first now will make it easier to pray first in the future.

Trivial or Monumental

Some trivial decisions may actually be larger than you think. Take what clothes we wear, for example. We think that it's trivial, but not necessarily. Wearing inappropriate clothing can cause us to be devalued by others, hinder us from sharing the Gospel, and give people the wrong impression about what kind of lifestyle we lead. This "little" decision can actually have a great impact. We should be praying about what we are wearing. Or how about what we eat? We usually sail through life thinking that food is not bad, and as long as we're not over-eating, we can eat whatever we want. But eating certain foods and drinking certain drinks can affect us. It affects how we feel, how we engage others, it affects our health and even affects our ability to be able to carry out the mission God might have for us. We will hit more on this in another chapter, but we should be praying about what we are eating. Now, I'm not talking about praying about if God is going to provide food and clothes for you as Jesus describes in Matthew 6. I'm talking about being intentional about making sure our trivial decisions are lined up with God's plan for our lives, too.

Honesty is the Best Policy

Did you know you can be honest with God? I mean, He already knows what you are really thinking, the good, the bad and the very ugly. Being honest with God about your problems, temptations, and confusion is exactly what He wants from us. Plus, He knows what it's like to be human. In a message to the students in our ministry, my husband enlightened our students with these words: "We are not approaching the throne of a God who cannot understand what it is like to be man."[16] He knows what it's like to be tempted, He knows what it's like to have people hate Him, He knows what it's like to hurt, He knows what it's like to be human. He understands us, which is why He can be our High Priest. And He hates lies, so there's no point in trying to lie about what you are feeling. And did you know Jesus actually knows we are only human? Seems like a simple concept, I know. He knows there's no way for our finite minds to understand all of His infinite thoughts and ways, so asking questions is an important part of communicating with the Lord.

Believe it or not, Siri does not have all the answers. Alexa doesn't either. But, friends, we know the One who does. What a privilege it is to be able to approach the One who holds the world in His hands. What a privilege to have an audience with the King. Church girls, don't wait to start having intimate conversations with the Lord. He has so much He wants to hear from you, and you have so much to hear from Him.

Pray first,

Holly

Make it Stick, Church Girl

1. After reading the greatest example of prayer, what part of your prayer life is lacking or maybe even non-existent?

2. What do you find to be the hardest part of prayer?

Sometimes writing your prayers can help you express what you want to tell Jesus. It also allows us to go back and see all that God has done as well as how your prayer life has grown more intimate.

3. I'm going to assume we all struggle with anxiety in some form. Read Matthew 11:28-30. What promise do we have from Jesus in these verses?

    We carry heavy loads. Whether it's sin, guilt, stress, school, career, relationship struggles, or any other of our 99 problems, we all carry heavy loads that burden us. Take time now to lay them at the feet of Jesus who promises you rest.

4. Who or what do you usually go to for answers before you go to the Lord?

5. Are there seemingly trivial parts of your life you should be praying about? Explain.

Dear Church Girl, Grudges Look Ugly on You

I'm struggling to write this one. I have been transparent through all these chapters and have loaned my experiences and failures to you with little hesitation, in hopes that you choose to learn from them. The stories of forgiveness in my life, however, do not just affect me. For me, the ones who have hurt me the worst are ones that I have built relationships with and love. I believe exploiting their faults for all to read would be counterproductive to the topic at hand, as well as hurt a lot of people. Nevertheless, there have been several times in my life where the mercy given to me demanded forgiveness that seemed impossible to give.

Because He Forgave Us

First off, we have got to understand why we are called to forgive in the first place. Remember when you were a little kid and you were given rules that you didn't understand. Our parents would say, "Because I said so." We hated it. We wanted a reason why we couldn't play in the rain or run outside barefoot or the reason we had to eat all our vegetables or shouldn't listen to loud music. Otherwise, we were following rules just to follow them, and we hated that, too. Scripture tells us to forgive others. Plain and simple. But do you understand why we are to forgive?

My mom has taught Kindergarten at a Christian school for over 20 years. Bless her. It takes a very special person to feel called to a position like this for so long. Shout out to all the teachers of the littles, a job I couldn't do. Anyway, one of the first verses my mom teaches her class and instructs them to memorize is Ephesians 4:32:

Be kind and compassionate to one another, forgiving each other, just as in Christ God forgave you.

We are called to forgive because He forgave us. Think about it. Jesus Christ suffered a terrible death, mocked, beaten, and scourged, and shed His blood so that we could be forgiven. In fact, Hebrews 9:22 tells us that *"...without the shedding of blood there is no forgiveness."* Jesus voluntarily gave His life, so that we could be forgiven. The real kicker? He was perfect. He never needed forgiveness because he never hurt feelings or abandoned people. He never cheated or manipulated. He was perfect, and yet He was the one willing to die for our eternal forgiveness. And, he commands us to forgive. If we are Christ followers, we are called to lay aside our selfish desires, take "me" off the throne of our hearts, and forgive others -- because He, perfect and holy, forgave us.

We also know that, as Christ followers, we should be reflecting the Lord and His character, and, trust me, His character is smothered in mercy and forgiveness. Psalm 86:5 says:

You, Lord, are forgiving and good, abounding in love to all who call to you.

Forgiveness is not just something the Lord does, but it is also part of who He is. It's His character. Micah 7:18 says:

Who is a God like you, who pardons sin and forgives the transgression of the remnant of his inheritance?

If we are going to reflect the character of our Lord so others can see, we must cultivate a lifestyle of forgiveness because it is very much in His character.

God's Word also tells us that to receive forgiveness of our sins, we must also forgive. Obviously forgiving others is important to Jesus. He even rather bluntly tells us later in Matthew 6:14-15 that:

If you forgive other people when they sin against you, your heavenly Father will also forgive you. But if you do not forgive others their sins, your Father will not forgive your sins.

Ladies, it doesn't get more straightforward than this, spoken from the mouth of Jesus Himself. By forgiving others, we are giving what we have been given and reflecting the character of our Savior. The mercy of Jesus demands forgiveness. And that, my friends, is why we are called to forgive.

What Forgiveness Doesn't Mean

Before we dive into what forgiveness means, I think it's important to address what it doesn't mean. It took a long time for me to figure this one out, but there was so much freedom once I caught on. I was a grudge holder, and, boy, did it look ugly on me. When others hurt, embarrass or lie to me, I tend to want to hold grudges. The pattern would go something like this: Someone would hurt me in some way. I would go home and vent, cry, and state the many reasons why they were wrong. I would neglect talking to them about it, and then I would ignore them, because there's no way I could make them think their actions were okay. And there it was, my biggest motivator for holding grudges. It would look like I'm approving of their wrongs. Seriously, that was it for me. I believed that forgiving others meant I was condoning their sin against me, and no way was I okay with them thinking what they had done wasn't a big deal. I thought that forgiving them and letting go of my grudge would belittle their wrongs. It would make less of what they had done to me, when, in fact, it was a big deal. This tendency has not miraculously disappeared, I'm only much better at recognizing it and intentionally letting it go.

Forgiveness is also not trust. Let me say that again. Forgiveness is not trust. In the words of my momma, "Forgiveness may be commanded, but trust is earned." Don't for one second think that after forgiving someone, you need to trust them, thus the age-old saying, "Fool me once, shame on you. Fool me twice, shame on me." Trust, respect, friendship, and reputation are all earned. Forgiveness does not mean trusting the one who wronged you.

Forgiveness doesn't mean condoning the sin. It doesn't mean making less of what has been done to you. It doesn't mean you don't have permission to hurt or feel. It doesn't mean you should let yourself be bullied. It doesn't mean you should bow to the decisions of others. It doesn't mean you should trust. It doesn't even mean you have to be best friends with your offender. Forgiveness is not these things.

What Forgiveness Means

So, what does forgiveness actually mean anyway? Dictionary.com defines forgive as "to grant pardon for or remission of [an offense or debt]."[17] Y'all, I'm not going to put on a front. Forgiveness is hard. When we are wronged, it is difficult to want to pardon the other person. Some of you reading this are battling abuses and offenses that are unspeakable. You have been hurt so much, with wounds so deep and scars so visible, it's a miracle you are able to stand on two feet and hold your head up. The thought of pardoning or releasing those who have abused, manipulated, abandoned, lied, cheated, and betrayed is straight-up gut-wrenching.

Forgiveness is not pardoning the sin but pardoning the person. It is releasing the person of bondage, so they can live in freedom and hopefully make better choices next time. And remember what I said about how forgiveness is not trusting the offender? While it's not trusting the guilty person, forgiveness is trusting the Lord. Letting go means we are completely trusting the Lord with the results and consequences. It is also trusting the Lord with the emotional effects that offenses and abuses can bring. When we let go of our grudges and choose forgiveness, we are choosing to trust the Lord with what is left of our pain and hurt. We are choosing to allow Him to heal us and our relationships. And, yes, it does cost us when we forgive. It can cost our feelings, our reputation, our time, and sometimes even our money. But think of what forgiveness cost Jesus? His life. It cost Him physical pain and suffering, His friends, money, and, ultimately, His life. When you look at it this way, it's easier to count our cost of forgiving as small, because we are not giving up nearly as much when we choose to forgive.

Grudges Are Ugly

Church girls, this is so true. Grudges are ugly. Someone embarrassed you in front of all your friends. Your best friend betrayed your trust. Your boyfriend cheated on you. Your parents are never there. Your professor belittles you. Someone sexually abused you. Your father left your family for another woman. We are imperfect people living in a sinful world, and we are wronged all the time, giving us plenty of chances to hold grudges. Holding a grudge means consistently having anger and resentment for someone who has done something wrong to you. And we layer grudge upon grudge and are left walking around with shoes of bitterness, jeans of resentment, a sweater of hostility, a necklace of indignation, and a hat of aggression. And, it's all kinds of ugly on us.

What we don't realize is that our grudges are not just affecting the offender. Our grudges are affecting us. You see, what it does is hold us captive and oppresses us. Instead of releasing the other person, we are holding ourselves in bondage. We become slaves to our resentment. And, the chains are heavy and shackles are tight. It consumes our thoughts, motivates a bitter attitude, drives resentful reactions, and, pretty soon, we are a slave to our grudge. Girl, it is ugly. I'm guilty, and there are two times in particular that I have refused to let it go for so long that others noticed my captivity. It affected my relationships with other people who had nothing to do with the situation. It affected my ability to minister and be used by God. It affected my personality and especially affected my relationship with the Lord. Trust me, it's not a good place to be. Eww. And, not exactly attractive.

Lewis B. Smedes once said, "To forgive is to set a prisoner free and discover that prisoner was you."[18] Forgiveness benefits us much more than those who have hurt us. It releases us from our grudge and allows us to surrender what has happened to the Lord. We are free from all the emotional and physical consequences that come with holding a grudge. Most importantly, it allows us to serve Jesus. When Jesus was giving His ever-famous Sermon on the Mount, He speaks to the people about storing up their treasures in Heaven. He ends this section by saying:

No one can serve two masters. Either you will hate the one and love the other, or you will be devoted to the one and despise the other. You cannot serve both God and money.
Matthew 6:24

Here, Jesus was speaking of serving the almighty dollar instead of the Lord, but the same principle applies. We cannot serve our grudge and God at the same time. Jesus is very clear; we cannot have two masters. Letting go of our grudges and choosing to forgive releases us to be able to serve one master, the Lord.

Grudges Also Cause Ulcers

Y'all, seriously. As much as holding a grudge can look ugly on you, it can also do some pretty ugly things to your body. Now, I know mental health is not often talked about in the church, but it's about time we give it some serious thought. Don't just take it from me. "A study from Emory University found that bitter people had higher blood pressure and were more likely to die from heart disease than more forgiving people."[19] When we are bitter, we stay in a fight mode that increases the C-reactive protein amount in our blood, thus increasing the chance of heart disease. "On top of that, prolonged feelings of resentment can also negatively impact metabolism, immune response, and organ function. Those feelings also put you at risk of developing depression and anxiety."[20] In another study conducted by the Medical College of Georgia found that "In a population-based survey, bearing grudges is associated with a history of pain disorders, cardiovascular disease, and stomach ulcers."[21] There's nothing like a grudge making you fat, sick, and depressed.

While my husband and I were flying from Atlanta to Punta Cana for a getaway, I saw a young woman with a very unique shirt. It read, "I'm allergic to haters. I breakout in forgiveness." It was refreshingly cute, and I loved it. You can get one on Amazon. You're welcome. But I thought long and hard about this shirt. Being a nurse, I know that an allergic reaction will cause an automatic histamine response in the body. Inflammation is "the local reaction of bodily tissues to injury caused by physical damage, infection, or allergic reaction,"[22] which is caused by the body's histamine reaction. Did you catch that? When there is damage or a foreign invader in our bodies, our automatic response is inflammation, which can also be a breakout. But, wouldn't it be nice if our automatic response to being emotionally hurt or damaged was forgiveness? I don't know about you, but that is exactly the kind of breakout I want to have when I am wronged. Grudges cause all sorts of ugly health problems. Do yourself a favor and learn now to let them go and breakout in forgiveness.

Repeat After Me: Vengeance is Not Mine

Sometimes we don't just hold grudges, but we also get even. We plot evil schemes of ways we can get back at others. That best friend who betrayed our trust? Now, we are going to share all her secrets on social media. That boyfriend who cheated on us? Now, we are going to sabotage every other relationship he has. That professor who belittled us? Now, we are going to make up accusations about him and make sure the dean finds out. Oh, and our parents who never pay attention to us? Now, we are going to find someone else who will pay attention to us, even if it is an unhealthy relationship. That will wake them up!

I frequently travel to Belize on mission with the students at our church. We visit remote villages where the houses have dirt floors and thatched roofs, the kitchen is outside over a fire, and a kid's entertainment is playing outside with scorpions and tarantulas. While visiting one year, my husband and I, along with several students from our church, sat down to teach a few Belizean teens to play Spoons. If you are not familiar with this card game, look it up. It's so much fun! The stack of cards must be shuffled after each round. After the first couple of rounds, it was my husband's turn to shuffle. Now, he's no professional dealer by any means, but he can shuffle a deck of cards quickly, probably like you have seen from many. These young people from Belize, however, had never seen anyone shuffle a deck of cards. They were mesmerized. So much so, that they all wanted to be the dealer. The game halted as one after another tried to shuffle the cards. And, watching their excitement while trying to learn to shuffle was maybe even more mesmerizing! Finally, my husband shuffled once more, so we could actually play the game.

God is the dealer, and He is the professional of all professionals. The wrongs of others will be dealt with by the Ancient of Days. The Lord is the dealer, not us. In Deuteronomy 32:35, the Lord says, *"It is mine to avenge. I will repay."* And, we are reminded once again in Romans 12:18-19:

If it is possible, as far as it depends on you live at peace with everyone. Do not take revenge, my dear friends, but leave room for God's wrath, for it is written: "It is mine to avenge; I will repay," says the Lord.

The problem is we want to be the dealer, just like those students in Belize. We want to do God's job and, for whatever reason, think we have the right to do so. But what did I say happened when the students began to try to be the dealer? The game stopped. We couldn't accomplish the game. When we try to be the dealer, the life we are supposed to be living, the life we are meant to live, halts. We can't move forward. Vengeance becomes our number one priority and everything else bows to its purpose. It all halts until we hand the cards back over to the Lord and let Him deal.

The Bible has a whole lot to say about taking revenge. Let's examine a few verses. Read them carefully.

Do not repay evil with evil or insult with insult. On the contrary, repay evil with blessing, because to this you were called so that you may inherit a blessing.
1 Peter 3:9

Make sure nobody pays back wrong for wrong, but always strive to do what is good for each other and
for everyone else.
1 Thessalonians 5:15

What? I'm not only told to refrain from revenge, but now you're asking me to bless them and do good to them? Yep. And we are following the example that Jesus gives of forgiveness. Yes, he died an awful death on the cross, showing us ultimate mercy, but he didn't stop at death. He rose victorious over death, hell, and grave, so that we could have freedom and eternal life. Life abundantly. This is grace. He forgives us and then gives us so much more. This is why we are not only called to forgive but to also love and bless in return. Talk about a difficult process.

Do not seek revenge or bear a grudge against anyone among your people, but love your neighbor as yourself. I
am the Lord.
Leviticus 19:18

And, church girl, I know you are probably already aware of this, but neighbor does not just mean those who live next to you or your besties. This is referring to everyone you come in contact with every day. We have got to take Elsa's advice and Let It Go! We have to give it to God and let Him deal. And you know what the most reassuring thing about letting go is? The Lord will deal with it. Erik Raymond reminds us that:

There are limits to human justice. We know that all kinds of wrongs go unpunished in this world. But, we take comfort in knowing that in the end, God will deal with everything in accordance with his inflexible justice, perfect wisdom, and eternal goodness. We can rest in this comfort, because we can rest in God.[23]

Young women, the Lord will judge. He will deal. Proverbs 20:22 instructs us to *"...wait for the Lord, and he will avenge you."* Be patient, friends. The Lord will avenge.

Jesus knew this as well. What I love is that Jesus did not just call us to refrain from revenge, he actually lived it out. He is, after all, our ultimate example. 1 Peter 2:21-23 says:

To this you were called, because Christ suffered for you, leaving you an example, that you should follow in his steps. "He committed no sin, and no deceit was found in his mouth." When they hurled their insults at him, he did not retaliate; when he suffered, he made no threats. Instead, he entrusted himself to him who judges justly.

While being unfairly accused, beaten, and led to a cross, Jesus did not retaliate. He did not threaten. And, did you catch that last part? "He entrusted himself to him who judges justly." Wow. Even Jesus let it go and gave it to His Father to judge. What an example we have in Jesus, our High Priest.

Giving it up and letting it go is hard, but vengeance is not ours. If we are not careful, we can quickly go from being the victim to making others a victim. We go from being sinned against to sinning against. Our innocence turns to guilt, and our dignity turns to shame. Let's learn to follow the example of our Savior, and let it go.

Forgive Them Again?

So, what about repeat offenders? What about the ones who do us wrong over and over and over again? We usually experience this with family members and close friends, whether it's absent or verbally abusive parents, boyfriends or husbands struggling with addiction, or best friends who can't keep their mouths shut. The ones we spend most of our time with are the ones who require much forgiveness.

My sister, my cousin, and I were quite a team growing up. We were all very close and spent a whole lot of time together. My sister was shy and distracted. My cousin and I were both very outspoken and determined. This all made things interesting, and we were constantly having to forgive each other -- constantly. For example, my sister, Kendall, would often get angry. She would even literally kick me when I went in her room to wake her up at the request of my parents. And, my cousin, Meghan, would often say what was on her mind, even if it hurt our feelings, while being quick to tell our parents if we did the same. And, I was no saint. Girl, I knew how to dish it out. I was sarcastic, stubborn, and willing to risk hurt feelings and relationships to make myself look better. The things we said to each other and the things we did to each other were terrible. We would intentionally embarrass and make each other feel less-than. All this happened again and again. And we had to forgive each other over and over. It's something we can look back and laugh at now, especially since we see this in our own children, but had we chosen not to continually forgive, our relationships would have become scarred and distant.

It's hard, but it's commanded. In Matthew we read that Peter came to Jesus and asks him how many times he should forgive someone who sins against him. He even gives Jesus a number. He says, *"Up to seven times?"*

Jesus answered, "I tell you, not seven times, but
seventy-seven times."
Matthew 18:22

Why did Jesus say this particular number, seventy-seven? Jesus was meaning that others should be forgiven a limitless about of times. There should be no limits to our forgiveness. Why?

Forgiveness is a thing of the spirit, a quality of the spirit.
All spiritual things, substances and realities – such as love,
mercy, grace, joy, forgiveness – cannot be measured or
limited. They are by their very nature spiritual and not
physical. Therefore, they are without measure or limit, so
they are to be known and practiced without
limit or measure.[24]

Our minds may remember how others have hurt us or wronged us, but the limitlessness of our spirits allows us to be able to forgive time and again. And that's exactly how the Lord forgives as well! It's limitless!

Reconciliation

I know what you're thinking. "Holly, you are crazy with a capital C if you think I'm going to reconcile my relationship with so and so." How can we be reconciled with those who have sexually abused us? Manipulated us? Murdered our family members? The answer is simple. Sometimes we can't. Reconciliation is changing the relationship from enemy to friendship. Let's face it, we don't exactly need to have a friend relationship with certain toxic people. Reconciliation also takes two people coming to an agreement to mend the relationship. But like I said, sometimes this just isn't possible. And, Paul knew all about this. Remember this verse from earlier in this chapter?

If it is possible, as far as it depends on you live at peace with everyone. Do not take revenge, my dear friends, but leave room for God's wrath, for it is written: "It is mine to avenge; I will repay," says the Lord.
Romans 12:18-19

Paul begins by saying, if possible. Sometimes, reconciling relationships just isn't possible; however, there is one reconciliation which is always possible. Take a look at these verses.

All this is from God who reconciled us to himself through Christ and gave us the ministry of reconciliation: that God was reconciling the world to himself in Christ, not counting people's sins against them. And he has committed to us

the message of reconciliation. We are therefore Christ's
ambassadors, as though God were making his appeal
through us. We implore you on Christ's behalf: Be
reconciled to God.
2 Corinthians 5:18-20

There is only one type of reconciliation this is talking about; our reconciliation to God, not each other. We have the message of reconciliation to God, a reconciliation that is always possible. That is the Gospel! Through the cross, Jesus made a way for us to be reconciled to God. Our relationship can change from being an enemy of God to being a friend of God. No matter who and no matter what sins committed, our job as ambassadors of Christ is to make sure others know how to be reconciled to the Lord and to implore, or urge, them to do so.

There is one more verse about reconciliation I want us to look at, and you've probably heard it before.

Therefore, if you are offering your gift at the altar and
there remember that your brother or sister has something
against you, leave your gift there in front of the altar. First
go and be reconciled to them; then come and
offer your gift.
Matthew 5:23-24

There are a few things you need to know about this verse. The words brother or sister are referring to someone from the same religious community as you, a believer. Secondly, notice that they have something against you. That means you have wronged them, not the other way around. You have sinned against them and, therefore, must go and reconcile the relationship before you worship or serve the Lord. Friends, don't ever expect the Lord to accept your gifts or offering or service if you have unconfessed sin in your life. He won't stand for it.

So, What I Mean is This...

Forgiveness is not easy. It has certainly not been easy in my life, at least. But it's a whole lot easier than holding a grudge. Church girls, it's time we start putting lies to rest about forgiveness. Let's throw away what forgiveness is not and claim what it really means, pardoning the sinner, not the sin, and trusting the Lord to handle it. Let's remember that a spirit of forgiveness is limitless, yet reconciliation may not always happen. And, please, please, let's remember that forgiveness from the Lord has already been handled, and reconciliation to Him is always possible. Paul's final words to the Corinthian church sum up the entire goal of forgiveness:

Finally, brothers and sisters, rejoice! Strive for full restoration, encourage one another, be of one mind, live in peace. And the God of love and peace will be with you.
2 Corinthians 13:11

This is our goal as believers, young women. To strive for restoration and live in peace with one another. Learn now to let go of your grudges and turn them over to the Ancient of Days. Cause, girl, they look ugly on you.

Grudges look ugly on you,

Holly

Make it Stick, Church Girl

1. Who do you need to forgive? Write their names below.

2. We explored Matthew 18:21-22 together already. Read the rest of the story in Matthew 18:23-35. The point Jesus is making is that we have been forgiven of so much, and our debt was settled on the cross. Because of this, we should forgive others when they sin against us.

3. Have you noticed grudges being ugly on you? If so, how? Resentment? Anger? Physical illness?

4. The mercy of Jesus demands forgiveness. What sins of yours has Jesus forgiven? Be detailed, and write some of them below.

5. In the story Jesus told, the man at the altar remembered someone he needed to be reconciled to because of a sin he had committed against them. I'm sure as you've read this chapter, the Lord has not only revealed those you need to forgive but also those you need to seek forgiveness from. What do you need to do to be reconciled to this person?

Dear Church Girl,
Keep Your Pants On

So, this is a vulnerable chapter for me. This is one that still hurts. This is the chapter I was so very reluctant to write but knew deep down in my soul needed to be told. It needed to be told because the struggle is real. The struggle is real and yet not supposed to be talked about. But that's a problem, you see, because when something is so inundated within our culture that it becomes a gross normalcy, shedding light on the truth is necessary. And, even though this chapter leaves me raw and exposed, the consequences of ignoring this struggle far outweigh my longing to keep my past hidden.

The Story

I was a sophomore in high school when it happened. You see, I had been in several relationships, but they were anything but very serious. But pitifully, I was the girl who always thought she had to have a boyfriend and always took it just far enough. Gross, I know. But it is what it is -- or was what it was -- whatever. Great, now I'm sounding like I'm a sophomore again. But when it happened, it really happened. I fell absolutely head over heels, hard and fast. Let me start at the beginning. I was in an elective group at school known as the ensemble. This group spent the school year learning music. We went to regional and state competitions, performed musicals, and learned many pieces of music from different eras. We also learned madrigal music and during the winter season would travel from place to place singing in our Renaissance costumes. This was pretty much the sum of my extracurricular life outside of school and church. Exciting, huh?

My parents learned very quickly that they were not going to be able to make it to many of my performances because there were just too many, and who wants to sit in the back of a fancy restaurant or event center listening to the same songs over and over again? So, they started asking around to see who would be willing to take me, the baby of the family, to all these events. They spoke with teachers and a lot of parents who were more familiar with the students in ensemble. They all reached the same conclusion. His name was Wes.

Now, let me tell you a little bit about Wes. He was crazy popular with students, loved by his teachers, and even all the parents had taken notice of him. He was polite, respectful, and responsible and in a "cool" kind of way. He was also voted "Most Courteous" in high school by his peers. Everybody loved Wes. Everybody still loves Wes. He was just an all-around great guy -- and still is. Oh, and then there's the fact that he was also a really good-looking guy. You see, he was not only in ensemble, he was also an athlete. He played varsity soccer all four years of high school, and he came with great hair and a six pack. So, you can imagine my delight when my parents told me the only way I could go to all the events was if Wes could drive me. I did have a boyfriend at the time, so my parents were not too concerned that I would fall so fast for this senior. Obviously, my parents had never seen him take off his shirt after soccer practice. But, allow me to continue.

He would pick me up in his Nissan Maxima and would have a little brown paper bag waiting on me. Ok, so it's not what you think. It was just Egg Nog. But I loved Egg Nog, so it meant a lot that he would even take notice and always have one waiting on me before every performance. It turns out he liked me, a lot. The Christmas season ended and, thus, the performances ended. I celebrated the holidays with my family and my boyfriend, who had no idea the feelings I had for this other guy. Our relationship inevitably ended by February, and on April 1, this very attractive and athletic senior asked me to be his girlfriend. My answer was a big, fat, excited "YES," and the rest is history. But there's a lot to that history. A lot of impulsivity, a lot of hurt, a lot of disappointment. We "declared" our love by April 12 and shortly after, we did it. We had sex. I was fifteen years old.

The Excuses

At first, I was excited with this new "love" I had experienced. It made me feel mature, like I clearly had my life together and was ready for the real world. It was fun, the sneaking around was adventurous, and I was just still so madly in love with him. I kept telling myself that it was ok because I loved him. It was ok because I knew we were going to get married anyway. It was ok because God knew the struggle and how attracted we were to each other. I mean, God created that desire and attraction, so He's really partly at fault here, right?

But then it happened -- conviction. And inevitably so because I was a child of God, a Christ follower. Conviction set in for both of us. I woke up with guilt every day for something I knew I could never take back. You may be thinking, "Holly, it's no big deal. Ask for forgiveness, renew your commitment, and then don't have sex again until you're married." Oh, how I wish it were that simple. The forgiveness was definitely there, but the consequences did not go away. It was hard. We knew we loved each other. We were insanely attracted to each other, and now we knew what it was like to be intimate with one another. That's the thing about sin. It entices you, pulls you in, and makes you want more. It will give you excuse after excuse, and eventually you start to believe the excuses are legitimate. We knew the right thing to do. We knew we needed to stop. But it was just so hard. And so, the cycle of sin and guilt continued for several months.

You see, I had made promises. Promises to Jesus. Promises to my parents. Promises to my future husband. Promises to myself. I went through the whole True Love Waits program, complete with ceremony, ring and tiara. It was a big deal. I made a promise to Jesus that I would remain pure because I had given my life to Him and His plans. I made a promise to my parents that I would follow through with abstinence obediently, knowing that they had my very best interests at heart. I made a promise to my future husband, that I would be able to purely give myself completely to him. And I made a promise to myself. I promised myself that I would not just give myself away. That I would be able to experience an amazing and gifted wedding night. A big problem was that I had already started giving little pieces of myself away to other guys. You know, taking it a little too far. It's not technically considered sex if your pants stay on, right? They just led me to, given the right moment, feel all the more comfortable taking it all the way. I had rationalized with myself so much that I believed my excuses to be valid reasons. But they weren't.

Yes, I loved Wes so much. Yes, I was almost certain I was going to marry him. Yes, I was fiercely attracted to him. And, yes, these may all be reasons, but there were no excuses. There were no excuses for breaking a promise I had made to my Creator, breaking a promise I made to my parents, my future husband, and myself. There were just no excuses. They seemed good enough before, but when it was all said and done, I was left with guilt, shame, disappointment and a longing for more, which would only bring me more guilt and shame and disappointment.

The Guilt

Why did I feel this guilty? I mean, I had sinned before, repented and gone on with life as normal, so what made this so different? After asking myself this over and over again, I finally realized two reasons the guilt was so strong. First, I knew that it completely went against God's intentions for sex. Genesis 2:25 tells us that *"Adam and his wife were both naked, and they felt no shame."* God intends for sex to be beautiful and meaningful, not shameful, and this only takes place when it is with the one you marry. And, God lets us know just how precious He views sex in marriage in Proverbs 5:15-19:

Drink water from your own cistern, running water from your own well....Let them be yours alone, never to be shared with strangers. May your fountain be blessed, and may you rejoice in the wife of your youth....May you ever be intoxicated with her love.

See, the Lord wants us to enjoy sex within the beautiful bond of marriage. Sex before marriage complicates God's intricate and detailed intentions, and we become confused about what sex is supposed to be. And, church girls, let me tell you, our society is feeding us a crazy, warped version of what God has intended all along. And, this version from culture gives us expectations that just are not real. The other reason for so much guilt is found in 1 Corinthians 6:18-20:

Flee from sexual immorality. All other sins a person commits are outside the body, but whoever sins sexually, sins against their own body. Do you not know that your bodies are temples of the Holy Spirit, who is in you, whom you have received from God? You are not your own; you were bought with a price. Therefore, honor God with your bodies.

My body was never mine to give. My body belongs to Jesus, the one who paid for me by dying on a cross. It wasn't my body to give away. Jesus wanted so much to give me completely to my spouse on my wedding night. Instead I chose to give it away myself, therefore desecrating the temple of the Holy Spirit. We are not our own! This is the whole point of surrender, young women.

The Brokenness

We kept our sexual sin a secret. Wes and I both told very few people, so my relationship with my parents never changed. My friends did not look at me differently, and my church friends and mentors had no idea what was going on. But, my relationship with Jesus was clearly broken, and it had been for a while. I was the girl who straddled the fence just enough to create an impressive balancing act, that is until I finally fell off the fence. My selfishness and greed for pleasure had caused me to put someone else on the throne of my heart -- myself. And now, while Jesus was chasing after me, ready to forgive, I was hiding in my shame. It's like I couldn't even look at Him. Couldn't even talk to Him. I was embarrassed, even though I knew He was already well aware of my state.

Do you know that sin separates us from God? Nothing separates us from His love, thank you, Jesus, but unconfessed sin causes a large space in our relationship with Him. Isaiah 59:2 tells us that *"your iniquities have separated you from your God."* It causes a distance that leaves us lonely and broken. The shame was great, and it took years to fully mend the relationship I had with the Lord. Please don't misunderstand. My eternal state was the same. I had repented and given my life to Christ in eighth grade, and no sin could take that away. But the relationship needed mending. It needed healing. And the healing took time. But God loves big and gives grace freely. I love to counsel students about this because I want to shout from the rooftops that you are not alone! You are not the only one struggling!

You don't have to be the "bad" girl with a promiscuous reputation to struggle with sexual desires or struggle to try to keep your sin hidden from God. You see, it's hard for the church girls too. We have a long list of "good" things that we do like going to church, leading worship, attending small group Bible study, being on the leadership team, volunteering at homeless shelters, and the list could go on and on. But the truth is none of us are good. We need rescuing from our sin just as much as the promiscuous girl next door, and our list doesn't change a thing. God's mercy does. There is complete restoration in Jesus Christ! He is ready to forgive and heal your relationship. *"If we confess our sins, He is faithful and just and will forgive us our sins and purify us from all unrighteousness"* (1 John 1:9). He loved us way too much to leave us broken!

The Not-so-Textbook Consequences

Ladies, please hear my heart. A few moments of pleasure are not worth the era of guilt that will follow. It's not worth the broken hearts, ruined relationships, stolen trust, and continual thoughts of what could have been. And you know what else? Most stories don't end up like mine. It's very unlikely your first serious relationship will be with the one you will marry. It's not worth the sexually transmitted diseases, unplanned pregnancy, abandoned friendships, dropping out of school, and the many other consequences that can come with having sex with someone other than your spouse.

Now, I'm certainly not going to dress up my story to make it more dramatic or make the consequences more severe. It could have been so much worse. I've seen it end up so much worse. I could have been pregnant at the age of fifteen. I could have contracted a sexually transmitted infection. I could have ruined my reputation in my school. I could have lost all trust my parents had in me. God's grace saw fit for me not to endure any of those natural punishments. So, what was my consequence? Mostly shame. I was left feeling guilty and unworthy. I also began to feel ashamed of my physical body. I felt like I had devalued myself. My self-esteem began to spiral downward into an abyss of insecurity that still haunts me today. I also started to compare myself to other girls. Was I good enough? Was I doing it right? Did he think about other girls the way he had just had me? Do I look attractive to him?

You see, it doesn't have to be what we view as severe consequences to interfere with our life. Just because we don't endure the textbook consequences doesn't mean we are in the clear. And do you know what? Society doesn't tell us about the not-so-textbook consequences of having sex before marriage. Even what may seem as the slightest of consequences can change the course of our future and even how we view ourselves. It can even taint how we think God views us. While I knew God would forgive me, this shame lied to me. This shame told me He would not want to use someone like me. And all of this because I didn't keep my pants on?

The Rest of the Story

So, how does the rest of the story go? How was I able to move on? Through much prayer, self-control, and setting boundaries, we were able to stop the cycle. Well, we allowed God to stop the cycle. There was so much grace, so much mercy. We decided we would intentionally be more careful with the situations we put ourselves in, and we took 1 Corinthians 7:9 to heart.

But if they cannot control themselves, they should marry, for it is better to marry than to burn with passion.

We began making plans to marry as soon as I graduated high school. Marrying so young is not what we usually counsel students to do, but it was exactly what was right for us. Somehow, making plans for our future, plans grounded on what God wanted for our life, made waiting a little easier. We definitely were not perfect, but grace abounded all the more. Wes was called into ministry, and we've now been very happily married for fifteen years and strive to serve Jesus every day. I know, fairy tale ending, right? But it took going through so much pain and guilt to get to that ending. And you know what? It wasn't necessary.

Many, if not most, of you reading this are church girls. You know -- the kids who have grown up faithfully in church and think this will never ever be an issue for you. Well, it will. If there hasn't already, there will be urges, desires, and thoughts. There will be guys with great hair and six packs. Don't let your guard down, and don't believe what society is telling you about sex. Sex was never meant to be a nonchalant hobby for us and the person we kinda like.

It is God's will that you should be sanctified: that you should avoid sexual immorality; that each of you should learn to control your own body in a way that is holy and honorable, not in passionate lust like the pagans, who do not know God.
1 Thessalonians 4:3-5

We were never meant to give ourselves away whenever we felt comfortable or deemed it the right time and person. And while society is telling us that it is normal, God tells us that sex with anyone other than our spouse is sin, plain and simple. Society tells us that if we use protection, we are free from the consequences of sex before marriage. But I am living proof that it is a lie.

It doesn't have to be this way for you. Learn from my mistakes. Learn from the mistakes of others around you. Trust me, this is not something you want to learn the hard way. Keep your pants on. I could dress up this phrase a bit. I could tell you to abstain from sex or wait for true love or pursue purity. But I prefer to keep it simple, easy to remember and straight to the point. Keep your pants on. And your shirt, for that matter, but you get the gist.

It's Not Just Sex...

While this chapter is about keeping our pants on and understanding the reasons we should remain sexually pure until marriage, we need to be sure we have a healthy understanding of Biblical purity. Sexual abstinence is only a small part of what it means to be pure. For a Christian, being pure means to have no moral defect or flaw. We read in the Old Testament that the sacrifice made for the atonement of sin were to be a spotless lamb. Pure. Blameless. The pure and innocent must shed blood in order for sins to be forgiven. Thus, why Jesus had to be pure and blameless to be worthy enough to shed His blood for our forgiveness. Romans 12:1 says:

Therefore, I urge you, brothers and sisters, in view of God's mercy, to offer your bodies as a living sacrifice, holy and pleasing to God--this is your true and proper worship.

We offer our bodies as living sacrifices, yet we are hardly pure. And, we already know we can't be perfect, right? So, what do we do? How do we cultivate a lifestyle of purity? First of all, we have to realize that we should be striving for purity is all aspects of our lives, not just our romantic lives. Are we making every effort to be pure or blameless in our speech? Our entertainment? Our leadership? Our driving? Our time? Our jobs? Our families?

Once we realize that purity is to be a part of every facet of our lives, we can look to Psalm 119:9-12 to tell us how to live a pure life. Ya'll, it point-blank asks the same question we are asking.

How can a young person stay on the path of purity?
By living according to your word.
Psalm 119:9

I know this seems like a simple request when you read it. Just do what the Bible says, right? But my life would prove otherwise. I'm sure you've noticed by now that I struggle with quite a bit when it comes to living according to the Word. How do we do that? How do we live according to His Word? We get our answer in the next few verses. Psalm 119:10 says:

I seek you with all my heart;
do not let me stray from your commands.

Notice that this verse puts some responsibility on us. We cannot expect to live lives of purity if we are not seeking what the Lord says about how we should live.

There are two spices I use on a very regular basis in my kitchen – cinnamon and cumin. I use cumin on my roasted squash and zucchini, baked whole chicken, cilantro-lime tilapia, and in our salsa. I use cinnamon in my coffee (it's actually really good) and on my roasted sweet potatoes. Oh, my, you can dice sweet potatoes and mix them with a little bit of EVOO, cinnamon, and sea salt, put them in the oven, and in about 45 minutes you have the most delectable side dish, crisp on the outside and gooey on the inside. And, the cinnamon makes all the difference. The problem, however, is that cinnamon and cumin are similar in color and texture. More times than I care to admit, I have sprinkled a generous amount of cumin on my sweet potatoes. I'll pick it up without reading the label and almost ruin them. I've also ruined squash and zucchini with the cinnamon. Yuck. But this is how we live our lives. What society is telling us is right or wrong is often disguised as the truth. We can't tell the difference unless we read the label, and the results are as gross as eating cumin on your sweet potatoes, except with more devastating consequences than just a bad taste. We've got to read the label. We must know the Word and seek truth. Seek it earnestly. God will not share our hearts with other things. When we start to truly seek Him and Him alone with all our hearts, living according to His Word will become easier.

Check out what the Psalmist says is another way to live a pure life:

I have hidden your Word in my heart,
that I might not sin against you.
Psalm 119:11

Look, I'm not going to beat a dead horse. We've already explored all the reasons why we must memorize Scripture and how it is our number one defense against temptation. But just know, ladies, when the Word is hidden in our hearts, it will help us in the most perilous and enticing of situations.

We are given one more way to living according to the Lord's Word, leading to a life of purity, in the very next verse.

> *Praise be to you, Lord;*
> *teach me your decrees.*
> *Psalm 119:12*

We have got to ask for it. Here the Psalmist is asking the Lord to teach him His Word. We must be so bold. We must lay down our pride and beg God to teach us. Instruct us. Reveal it to us. Explain it to us. Lord, please impart your wisdom on us, and teach us your Word. Paul tells us in 2 Timothy 2:22 to:

> *Flee the evil desires of youth, and pursue righteousness,*
> *faith, love and peace, along with those who call on the*
> *Lord out of a pure heart.*

Notice that in order to flee evil and pursue righteousness, the condition of our hearts is a key factor. After we flee, we then, out of pure hearts, ask of the Lord. The state of our heart matter most because our speech and actions are the outpouring of what is in our hearts. If our pursuit is to be like Jesus, then we need to pray for pure hearts. We cannot expect our lifestyle to be blameless if our hearts are tainted.

Want to live a life of purity in all aspects of your life? Live according to the Word by reading it, memorizing it, and asking the Lord to teach it. I'm guessing by now you're are recognizing a common theme throughout these letters. God's Word is so important.

Are You Stuck?

If you are reading this and are already stuck in the same cycle I was in, there is healing in Christ. There is so much mercy, and His forgiveness will overwhelm you, church girl. Find someone to hold you accountable, talk with a pastor or your parents, if you can, and set boundaries. And, if the person you are with wants nothing to do with waiting until marriage, the relationship needs to end until you both are on the same page and both are willing to wait. God has big plans for you, and If you are vulnerable to His forgiveness and mercy, His grace will abound!

Keep your parts on,

Make it Stick, Church Girl

1. What are the sexual sins you may be dealing with?
   Premarital sex? Taking it too far? Pornography?
   Promiscuity? Write them below or in a private journal.
   Confess these to Jesus. Speak candidly to Him. He
   already knows anyway, but telling Jesus that you know
   you struggle with these particular sins is a very
   important initial step to being restored.

2. Read Romans 8:1-4. What hope is given in these
   verses?

3. Now read Romans 8:5-13. If we are believers, we can
   be Spirit-led, but we must allow Him to lead. It's
   important to know that just because you have
   repented doesn't mean that the temptation and urges
   go away. They will always remain.

4. What are some practical ways to combat the
   temptation of sexual sin?

Never put yourself in a situation that would cause you to stumble, like being alone with your date. Also, be sure you set boundaries and know them well before you date. Once you begin dating, have these conversations with your boyfriend. Talk about these boundaries and what your expectations are. Also, talk about what triggers both of you to want to give in to temptation and come up with ways to avoid them. If the person you are dating doesn't want to have these conversations with you, pray about whether or not you should be dating them. Oh, and keep your pants on.

Dear Church Girl, Just Be Kind

When I was in my earlier years of middle school, I was hardly intentional about being kind, and, if I'm being honest, I was just downright mean. Y'all, I didn't even have a pleasant spirit. I had a very smart mouth as my momma would say, and it was not at all uncommon for sarcastic comments to spew forth. To put it bluntly, there were too many instances -- way too many for me to remember -- where my unkindness hurt others. There is one, however, I can't seem to forget.

We were on a middle school field trip and had stopped for fast food. There was a student in a grade below me who really struggled to fit in and, for lack of better words, was socially awkward. I took advantage of his struggle and decided to seize the opportunity to make myself look better at his expense. In front of everyone, I said, "Hey, if everything God made was good, then who made you?" Most everyone laughed, and I smirked, knowing I just gained some cool points with my peers. Truth is, I have a really hard time sharing this. Those words still haunt me over twenty years later, and I can't help but wonder if my blatant unkindness managed to seriously injure him for life. How could I speak such brutal and unkind words and then bring God into the picture by quoting scripture?

And, it does seem so fundamental. You know, just be kind to others, but I'm afraid I learned the importance of this truth and its meaning way too late in life. Being kind doesn't come naturally to me. Sure, I know that it doesn't necessarily come natural to any human, seeing as we are all born sinners, but there are plenty of people who do not know Jesus and are very kind to others, treating them the way they want to be treated. These people are usually born with sweet-spirited personalities of humbleness and meekness. But not me. I have a very matter-of-fact attitude with a "suck it up, buttercup" personality -- just ask my kids. And, like I've said before, sarcastic thoughts are usually still my first. While we definitely need people who are real and tell it like it is, that does not give us a free pass to toss the kindness card out the window. Instead, we must work harder at developing our kindness.

During our first leadership trip to SLU 101, we had to fill out a DISC profile. [25] This was a rather lengthy questionnaire that pinpointed what kind of personality you have. It unveiled not only your strengths but also your weaknesses. It was very humbling. My personality was dominant, like off-the-charts dominant. So, basically this was saying that I was a get-the-job-done kind of girl who was independent, strong-willed, competent and would take on any challenge. Sounds great, right? Well, then it began to lay out my weaknesses right there in front of my face. Actually, right there in front of 400 other people. I'm terrible at showing patience and being sensitive to others. I forget to build relationships because I'm so focused on getting the job done, and my mouth will most likely be what gets me in trouble. Great. What was I supposed to do with this? Well, like any other get-the-job-done girl would do, I set a goal to be intentional about making my weaknesses stronger. Ladies, we do not have a free pass to let our weaknesses remain our weaknesses. For me, I had to work harder at building relationships. I had to work harder at being patient. I had to work harder at being kind.

And, we have got to be intentional about this. If we are Christians, we already have kindness. Kindness is a fruit of the Spirit, which we received when we surrendered to Christ, so we definitely already have it. The problem is that we just don't use it. Maybe we don't use it because we think it's just not in our personality. Maybe we don't display it because we think we don't actually struggle with having kindness. Or maybe we don't because it's just too hard. My excuse was definitely a combination of all three, but I eventually learned that I really needed to train myself and unlearn a few things. Before we dive into how we can train ourselves in kindness, it's important for us to understand what kindness is and why we should be kind in the first place.

What is kindness? What does it mean to be kind? Kindness is defined as "the quality of being friendly, generous and considerate."[26] Basically, just be nice, right?

This usually comes from our actions. Use words that will build up and not tear down. Let others go before you. Do favors without expecting anything in return. Smile at people. Encourage and compliment others. These are ways we show kindness, ways we show we are friendly, generous and considerate. Let's face it. Sometimes we just have to get back to the basics and be reminded of lessons we should have learned in kindergarten. To put it simply, kindness is a reflection of our love. It is often how we show people we love them. But why? Why should we show kindness to others? I believe there are two primary reasons to show kindness to others. First of all, like we learned from my first letter to you, we are chosen.

Therefore, as God's chosen people, holy and dearly loved, clothe yourselves with compassion, kindness, humility, gentleness and patience.
Colossians 3:12

We are chosen. As Christians we are called to be set apart and showing kindness to each other sets us apart from the rest of the world. God has chosen us to bear His name and make His name great, and he expects us to do it with kindness. We don't show kindness to earn brownie points with God or work our way to the top, so to speak. We show kindness as an outpouring of obedience to our Savior, who gave everything for us. We show kindness because we have been chosen.

Another reason we should show kindness is because others are watching.

Dear friends, since God so loved us, we also ought to love one another. No one has ever seen God; but if we love one another, God lives in us and his love is made complete in us.
1 John 4:11-12

We bear the name of Jesus, and, like it or not, how we treat others will either hurt His name or build it up. Others are watching. The only way for others, including the lost, to see the love of Christ is by our love. He doesn't say they will know because we carry a Bible or sing in the choir or wear a Christian t-shirt or hold the title of a Pastor's wife or because we are church girls. He says they will know by our love. And we very well can't express love for one another without being kind. God's Word tells us to:

Be devoted to one another in love. Honor one another above yourselves. Never be lacking in zeal, but keep your spiritual fervor, serving the Lord.
Romans 12:10-11

At all times and to all people, we are called to be fervent in Spirit. And, guess what? The Holy Spirit provides us with kindness. It's part of the fruit of the Spirit. We are given kindness from the Holy Spirit, and God expects us to put away our excuses and be kind to others. Galatians 5:22-25 says:

But the fruit of the Spirit is love, joy, peace, forbearance, kindness, goodness, faithfulness, gentleness and self-control. Against such things there is no law. Those who belong to Christ Jesus have crucified the flesh with its passions and desires. Since we live by the Spirit, let us keep in step with the Spirit.

The Greek word for kindness here is chréstotés, which means "goodness, excellence, uprightness."[27] In order to keep in step with the Spirit, we are to act with excellence, gentleness, and goodness toward others. And this can be oh so hard when we don't naturally have that sweet personality that others have. It can also be hard when we just don't feel like being kind, whatever the reason may be. And, oh, the excuses we will give. You know the "forgive what I said when I was hungry" type of excuses? The Bible doesn't say to be kind when others are kind. It doesn't say to be kind to everyone except those in your family. Jesus doesn't tell us to be kind unless you've had a bad day. God doesn't expect us to only be kind when things are going smoothly and as planned.

Especially Those

While driving home from school, my eight-year-old daughter was very upset. She said another student in her class had lied to her. She went on and on about how lying was bad and how this particular student was such a "mean person" because of his deceit. I quietly replied, "Baby girl, how many times have you lied to me?" There was a long pause. Very frustrated, she finally said, "That's different! You're my family!" I questioned why she thought she was justified in treating her family worse than other people, to which she had no reply. Point made, for now, at least. After all, we are all a work in progress.

And I do have this hope, way down in the pit of my soul that my kids really do love each other. I think. Well, let's be honest, most of the time I can't tell. One minute they're playing with each other with the biggest grins and giggles. And, then the next minute they might as well be in a boxing ring; at least I think it would be safer in a boxing ring. You know, safer if they wore mouth guards and were hitting each other with padded gloves instead of bare fists or large nerf guns. But the truth is, I just can't tell if they really love each other.

I see striking similarities in my children and the church. Now, I'm not talking about the church we attend every Sunday, but I am referring to the church as a whole, as in all believers, which would include your church, my church -- and me. Many times, we are like my children. The world just can't quite tell if we love one another. Our world is full of hatred, selfishness, pride, and downright meanness. And, sad to say, much of it is coming from believers. Whether it's losing our patience in the parking lot after service because we are late for lunch or ignoring another Christian because they don't fit into our "group." Or how about gossiping about other young women and calling it a "prayer request"? These are just a few examples of how we deny love to our own people. God's own people. Galatians 6:10 says:

Therefore, as we have opportunity, let us do good to all people, especially those who belong to the family of believers.

Especially. This is so crucial because the world is certain not to want anything to do with our Jesus if His people can't even seem to be kind to one another. The message is simple, and the application is hard, I know. It's easier to be unkind to the ones we love and are most comfortable around. But the world needs to see that we are kind to each other. But being kind is hard sometimes. And, believe it or not, being kind is harder for some than others. For me personally, I've had to work hard at learning to be kind, and sometimes I had to learn the hard way.

Why should we love one another? So, our world will be able to tell we belong to Jesus. Our love for one another should mimic the way Jesus loves us -- with kindness. This also gives the world glimpses of how Jesus loves them. Of course, this in no way means we shouldn't show love to everyone, even those who don't believe. That command is given all over scripture, but it's imperative that the church love each other. In his must-read book, *Chasing Elephants*, Brent Crowe, Ph.D. writes that "The reputation of the church is largely determined by how Christians treat each other."[28] What has neglecting to be kind to other believers done to our individual reputation? To the church's reputation? To Jesus' reputation?

And this is actually a pretty big deal. Why? Jesus answers this question in the book of John. Jesus is preparing for His death. They have just taken part in the last supper with their Lord. And Jesus says:

A new command I give you: Love one another. As I have loved you, so you must love one another. By this all men

will know that you are my disciples, if you love one
another.
John 13:34-35

This was one of the last commands Jesus gave His disciples. Obviously, Jesus knew we would struggle to show love for even other sisters in Christ. He knew we would struggle to be kind. Thankfully, He promises His disciples later that He will send His Spirit to counsel us, to help us. And it's this same Spirit we read about in Galatians, giving us His fruit, of which kindness is among. Along with telling us about the fruit of the Spirit, Paul is sure to let us know that this fruit does not come natural for us. We are sinners. Our flesh desires the exact opposite of the Spirit. Therefore, in order to add kindness to our lifestyles, some things have to be removed. Take a look at what Ephesians 4:31-32 says:

Get rid of all bitterness, rage and anger, brawling and
slander, along with every form of malice. Be kind and
compassionate to one another, forgiving each other, just
as in Christ God forgave you.

Notice what we are supposed to do before we are kind to others. We are to get rid of bitterness, rage, anger, brawling, slander, and every form of malice. The Greek word for malice literally means badness. We've got to get rid of whatever ways we are showing badness in order to be kind and compassionate. In other words, we cannot be kind and bitter at the same time. We cannot participate in a fit of rage and be kind at the same time. We must get rid of the badness to show the goodness to others. I encourage you to think about what it is you need to get rid of in order to be kind. Praying through and removing those things might be just what you need in order to cultivate kindness into your lifestyle. This brings me to a different translation of kindness we read about in God's Word. Do you remember what I said about kindness usually coming from our actions? Kindness also comes from our reactions. We can also call this mercy.

Loving-Kindness

We show this kindness because we have been shown the ultimate kindness. We have received a kindness from Jesus that surpasses all amounts of kindness. It's a kindness that denies self and comfort to benefit us. It's a kindness that, even in our wretched state, was given so freely to save us from eternity without our Lord. We are called to be kind because the Lord is kind to us, showing mercy to us. The Hebrew word for kindness is checed, which is also defined as "merciful kindness."[29] This type of kindness comes from our reactions. It comes from our responses, if you will.

We are given a remarkable example of this type of kindness in 2 Samuel 9. Before David was king, he was pursued by King Saul. He wanted to kill David, clearly jealous of the fact that God had stripped him of his throne and given it to David. He tried multiple times to no avail. David, however, had several opportunities to kill Saul and instead spared his life. Meanwhile a strong friendship had formed between Saul's son, Jonathan, and David, so close a friendship that it led to David making a promise to

Jonathan that he would show *"unfailing kindness like the Lord's kindness"* to the house of Saul always (1 Samuel 20:14). Fast-forward many years later, after Saul and Jonathan's death, David sits with his kingdom established, riches abounding, and all is good. 2 Samuel 9:1 says that David asked, *"Is there anyone still left of the house of Saul to whom I can show kindness for Jonathan's sake?"*

Y'all. Let this sink in. This one verse absolutely blows my mind. David literally has everything he could ever want or ever need at his fingertips. His kingdom is secure and successful, and yet he is still not content to just bask in his riches. Instead he intentionally seeks someone to whom he can be kind. Just think about the difference we could make for the kingdom of God if we woke up every morning intentionally looking for someone to be kind to? To show mercy to? And, not just that. What about intentionally looking for someone from our enemy's family to be kind to?

This checed type of kindness is not just merely being nice to someone but actually showing the kind of loving-kindness that God shows to us, full of mercy and grace. And this next part makes us appreciate this account of David even more. David is told of a son of Jonathan who is lame in both feet. He doesn't just merely send him a message, but David seeks him out and has him brought to him. His name was Mephibosheth. Upon meeting David, Mephibosheth bows down and says, *"What is your servant, that you should notice a dead dog like me?"* Mephibosheth knows there is nothing he can give David. He has nothing to offer. He is lame in both feet, and his social status is far from elite. And he knows it, which is why he refers to himself as a dead dog in the presence of the king.

We are Mephibosheth. It is crucial we realize this. We have an Almighty King, who is full of power and has anything He wants at His fingertips. Who are we in the sight of the Father but a dead dog? We are nothing. We are useless. So, God decided to show His loving-kindness, this same type of kindness David shows. He sent His only Son to die in our place and rescue us from the sinful state along with its eternal consequences. Titus 3:4-5 says:

But when the kindness and love of God our Savior appeared, he saved us, not because of righteous things we had done, but because of his mercy.

David did not show kindness because of anything Mephibosheth did or said. And the Lord does not show us kindness because of anything we have done. It is all because of His character of mercy. Godly mercifulness produces kindness. The type of kindness that causes others around us to stop and stare. David gives everything once belonging to Saul to Mephibosheth. He gives him the land for his servants to farm and gives him a spot at the king's table. Wow! Mephibosheth is given a permanent seat at the king's table. He doesn't earn this seat, nor does he bargain for this seat. It is freely given to him because of the kindness David chooses to show. And, it's the same for us. We did absolutely nothing to earn a permanent seat at God's table. We did nothing to earn our place as heirs and children of the Almighty King. Instead it was freely given to us because of the kindness of our Lord. But here is what's crucial. We must understand that we are Mephibosheth in this account. We can't show this type of loving-kindness to others until we fully grasp that we were a dead dog who has been shown mercy. Only then can we extend this same kindness to those around us.

So how do we do this anyway? How do we change the way we live to cultivate a life where we wake up asking to whom we should show kindness? I'm obviously not an expert on this, but I found several things to be helpful for me. First of all, make sure you are a Jesus follower. This may sound silly given the title of this book, but do you know that story I shared earlier about being unkind to my classmate at school? At that time in my life, I had not truly made the decision to follow Christ. I thought I was saved. I went to a Christian school, came from a family of preachers, and played the church game, but I was lost. Make sure you have a relationship with Jesus. You may be unkind because you don't have the Holy Spirit who gives us kindness. If you are not a Christian or are unsure about what it means to follow Christ, stop reading this chapter now and turn to *I Was but Now* at the end of this book. So, how else can we be intentional about fostering a lifestyle of kindness?

Pray. If you are sure you have accepted Christ as your savior, then pray. Ask God to reveal ways you show unkindness or areas where you struggle to be kind. When we pray with sincere hearts, God hears, and He is eager to give us the desires of our heart, especially when it aligns with His heart. And we know that learning to show kindness obviously aligns with God's heart because He commands us to do so! Persistently pray for God to reveal your sin and for God to help you show kindness -- His kind of mercy-giving kindness. Pray that God reveals people, enemies even, to whom you need to show loving-kindness. Ladies, I had to do this. I had to beg the Lord to show me how to be kind and give me more of a mercy-heart.

Be intentional. Make a list of your excuses for being unkind and pray over them. Ask God to loose the chains keeping you from being kind or showing mercy. Maybe you need to forgive someone first. Maybe you need to change your friend group. Maybe you need to ask the Lord to reveal why you are being unkind. Also, make another list. This time make a list of people who need your kindness. This will help you be intentional. Find a journal or planner or digital app that allows you to take notes and write the names of those who need extra kindness or encouragement. Personally, when someone approaches me about a prayer request or struggle or they just look like they are having a terrible week, I will write their name down in my planner after my encounter with them. Then, when I sit down to plan my week, I take those names and pray over them and text them the next week. But everything is planned because I have to be intentional. And, you are not too young to do this! This isn't done because I am older but because I am intentional. You can also put a note by your bed to remind you to ask yourself the question David asked himself every day: Who can I show kindness to? There's another important way to help us cultivate a life of kindness.

Shut up. Way too often we run our mouths before we even think. If you are anything like me at all, you struggle with saying the first thing that pops in your head. But, c'mon. We know that the first thing we think is usually not the best thing to say. We've also got to learn the art of listening. Before I know I'm going to have an encounter with someone who may be hard to show mercy to, I pray and ask the Lord to help me listen. Listening is naturally not my first response. If we'd learn to shut up and listen, take a few moments, and then respond, we could be more intentional about being kind. We've got to stop letting our mouths get us in trouble.

It took way too long for me to realize the significance of intentionally showing kindness in my everyday life and making it a lifestyle. While the damage that was done with my hateful words, sarcasm, or pure meanness can't be erased, I now choose to be intentional about being kind. Still not perfect, but intentional. When I think of the relationships I could have formed, the friendships made, the productive conversations I could have taken part in, the number of people I could have shared God's love and His Gospel with, it brings me such regret, remorse, and disappointment. Because you know what? They won't listen without kindness. Try making friends without kindness. It doesn't work. Try building relationships with anyone without kindness. It doesn't work. Try sharing the Gospel without kindness. It just doesn't work, and they just won't listen, plain and simple. Time to get intentional, church girls. Time to just be kind.

Just be kind,

Make it Stick, Church Girl

1. Do you struggle with kindness when it's an action or a reaction? Explain.

2. Write a list of excuses you give for being unkind below.

3. Write a list of people who need some of the Jesus-kind-of-loving-kindness (mercy) from you below.

4. Pray over your list daily, and ask God to whom you should show kindness.

5. Rest in the fact that the Lord forgives. He forgives us when we are unkind, and he will heal our past of unkind words and choices.

Dear Church Girl, Your Health Actually Matters

Did you know that God wants to use us? He really does. He doesn't need to, but He actually wants to. Just think about it. The God who created the universe, the one who placed the stars in the sky and formed this earth we are so fascinated with, wants to use us for His glory. To build His kingdom. That's a pretty overwhelming concept to grasp. But there is nothing more sobering, more frightening, than to think that we are used by an almighty God to fulfill His plans. And that He chooses to use us. Wow. He is all powerful. He is all knowing. He is completely and utterly enough, yet He chooses to use us. And I don't know about you, but I want to be used. I want God to use me, but I can look back on times in my life where He had to use someone else instead because I wasn't willing or prepared to be used. Yes, many times I wasn't fit emotionally or spiritually to be used. But, for the sake of this chapter, we will focus on not being fit physically.

We Are the Temple

Now before you close the book and shout that we are enough no matter what, let's remember that we are not enough. We never will be. That is why we need a Savior. We are not enough, but Jesus is. And, while God can use anyone if He wills, could it be that He is not trusting us with more because we are not taking care of our bodies? I mean, if we can't take care of our own bodies, how are we to care for others? I know this is a topic that the church doesn't talk about much, but the kings and queens of potlucks don't want to talk about it. Shocker, I know. Caring for our temples is an uncomfortable topic because so many struggle with it. If preachers of God's Word struggle with taking care of their bodies, God's temple, then they certainly can't preach about it, right. Wrong. It is important. And it's time we stop ignoring the fact that the church doesn't want to talk about our physical health.

Let's first talk about the purpose of the temple. God told the Israelites to build a tabernacle so He may dwell among His people. It was to be a place of sacrifice and repentance, worship and prayer, and fellowship among believers. In Exodus 25:8, God tells Moses to have the Israelites *"...make a sanctuary for me, and I will dwell among them."* He goes on to tell them to do it exactly as He commands them. The rest of Exodus is full of instructions on how to build the tabernacle, what to put in the tabernacle and how to furnish it, right down to the color and length of curtains. The rest of Exodus is literally chapters of how to build and take care of the tabernacle, along with revealing its purpose. And, after all this was accomplished and Moses did everything the Lord commanded, the glory of the Lord filled the tabernacle. Wow! What a sight that would have been - to watch the glory of the Lord descend in a cloud. Long story short, when the Israelites arrived in the Promised Land (finally), Solomon builds a more permanent dwelling place for the Lord, the temple. He builds it using the finest of materials, including cedars from Lebanon and pure gold, and it was furnished with bronze and gold finishes.

And when the temple was rebuilt, Ezra tells us it was done with diligent work. Obviously, God cared about His dwelling place.   Fast forward to the day of Jesus' Resurrection, and we learn that we are now the temple, our bodies. We are God's dwelling place, displaying His glory, or at least that is supposed to be our purpose.

Please, Don't Misunderstand

What I am not saying: I am not at all trying to imply that how we take care of our physical bodies has any kind of redemptive work. Eating keto and going to your CrossFit class twice a week does not make you any more Christian than the couch potato eating leftover chicken casserole from the church's potluck last night. It is through the blood of Jesus alone. Alone. Not Jesus and paleo. Not Jesus and yoga. Not Jesus and essential oils. Not Jesus and eight hours of sleep. It's through Jesus alone that we are saved, and we better darn well be careful if we think we need to add something to His blood. That's dangerous ground.

What I am trying to say: While taking care of our physical bodies does not benefit us for redemption or salvation, it does make us more fit to be used. It prepares us for His work. For instance, if I feel God is calling me to be a missionary in Haiti but I have lung cancer from 20 years of smoking, I've forfeited the chance to serve in that capacity. God may find someone else and use them instead. We will dive deeper into what this means, but hopefully you get the gist. Robby Gallaty, pastor of Long Hollow Baptist Church, spoke about the importance of taking care of your health to a large gathering of student pastors and workers. Obviously, we struggle too. In his sermon he said, "If our body is a temple of the Holy Spirit, we are only as good as our health allows."[30]

Now, I know that some things are completely out of our control. Sometimes God allows things to happen to us, even physically, so that He can use us to reach those we might not otherwise be able to or so that His glory and strength is made known through our weaknesses. We read about this when Paul tells us of the thorn in his flesh. He says, "I delight in weaknesses, in insults, in hardships, in persecutions, in difficulties. For when I am weak then I am strong" (2 Corinthians 12:10). Other times, however, things happen because we don't take care of our bodies, and there are consequences for it. Paul never tells us to delight in our sin. But that's exactly what neglecting to take care of your body is -- sin. When we are filling our bodies with junk, when we become addicted to food or alcohol, when we are lazy, when we deprive our bodies of what it needs, we are sinning. In light of this, we should make every diligent effort to be fit physically, spiritually, mentally and emotionally for the service of God.

I know this seems so out of place for a book written especially for young women, but if you only knew. If my thirty-three-year-old self could go back and tell my eighteen-year-old self a thing or two, the importance of being physically healthy would definitely be on the top of the list. The decisions you make now when you are young and the habits you form will either hinder or help your readiness and availability to be used by God. And it's important now more than ever due to the culture in which we live. Our bodies are to be set apart for God's use. I truly believe setting yourself apart means taking care of your physical body.

Slaves to Indulgence or Freed to Serve?

Here's the kicker. We are slaves to our culture. This culture of indulgence and convenience, which has led us to over-eating and being lazy, has made us slaves. For example, my husband and I spent 6 days away together at an all-inclusive resort in the Dominican. This place is full of all-you-can-eat buffets, unlimited beverages, room service at any hour and fresh beach towels to swap at every outing to the pool or beach, which is lined with limitless Bali beds and sun chairs, along with waiters ready to serve you. It really is awesome for a week-long vacation, but it is scary close to our culture here in the states. We strive to be able to over-indulge and are willing to go into debt or work 70 hours a week to make those indulgences happen. I'm all about vacating and being lazy for a week or so, but our convenience-driven mindset cannot be an everyday lifestyle. You see, we tend to find happiness, comfort and fulfillment in food or laziness, but we must find it in Jesus. Paul addresses this very issue head-on in 1 Corinthians.

"I have the right to do anything," you say – but not everything is beneficial. "I have the right to do anything" – but I will not be mastered by anything. You say, "Food for the stomach and the stomach for food, and God will destroy them both." The body, however, is not meant for sexual immorality but for the Lord and the Lord for the body. By his power God raised the Lord from the dead, and he will raise us also. Do you not know that your bodies are members of Christ himself?... Do you not know that your bodies are temples of the Holy Spirit, who is in you, whom you have received from God? You are not your own; you were bought at price. Therefore honor God with your bodies.
1 Corinthians 6:12-20

Paul is addressing the issue of sexual immorality with the church in Corinth, but the same can and should be applied to anything that holds us captive. We are not to be mastered by anything. Why? Because Jesus has already bought us. And because of this, we should be honoring God with our bodies.

Another reason for honoring God with our bodies? Remember, we are chosen. You are *"God's special possession, that you may declare the praises of Him who called you out of darkness and into his wonderful light"* (1 Peter 2:9). We are to be set apart for God's use because we are his special possession. And, Paul tells us that because of this, *"...let us purify ourselves from everything that contaminates body and spirit, perfecting holiness out of reverence for God"* (2 Corinthians 7:1).

A third reason for honoring God with our physical and spiritual self is because we were created to do the work of Jesus. Stay with me. Ephesians 2:10 says, *"For we are God's handiwork, created in Christ Jesus to do good works, which God prepared in advance for us to do."* God has a purpose and a plan for our lives, just like with Jesus. Jesus said He came to do the will of His Father, and He did it perfectly because, well, He's perfect. We are set apart to do the will of our Father. The problem is that we are not perfect. We can actually mess up His will for our lives. Don't get me wrong. God is sovereign, but we must not confuse His will and His sovereignty. God has a sovereign plan for redemption and the end of the beginning that no one can thwart. He will use whatever and whomever to make it happen. Scripture tells us, however, that it isn't God's will for anyone to perish, but people are perishing every day. It is also not God's will for us to sin, but here we are, sinning every day. In other words, if it is not God's will for us to sin, then it is not in God's will for us to overeat, deprive our bodies of nutrients, be lazy, smoke or become addicted to anything because it makes us less fit to serve and be used by God. If Kim in Asia needs to hear the Gospel, but we are too unhealthy to fly oversees and share it with her, God will use someone else to bring the Gospel to Kim. But, don't we want Him to use us? Or, maybe our friend, John, needs help overcoming his sin of pornography. God would like to use us but has to use someone else because we are so tired from always staying up late to binge Netflix that we can't effectively minister to him. And heaven forbid, no one tells Kim about Jesus or helps John out of his bondage before it's fatal for them. Obviously, there's some tension to this concept.

God is God. He has no limitations. I am not saying we are limiting God, but, rather, we are limiting ourselves. Remember, the Lord does not need us. If He can make animals talk (Numbers 22) to accomplish what he wants, He certainly will get the job done one way or another. No, he doesn't need us, but He wants to use us. And, sometimes, in His grace, God allows us to be used despite our poor planning, lack of discipline, and inept desire to care for our bodies. But don't think for one second that He will not use someone else instead.

So, What Do We Do?

So, how do we combat this? How are we supposed to fight this desire for indulgence that leads to neglecting our bodies and, in turn, neglecting the work of the Lord? If any of our choices make us less fit for service, we should fight it with the Holy Spirit. When Jesus was tempted in the desert, He used Scripture to fight against temptation. The Holy Spirit reveals Scripture and its meaning to us, allowing it to be used during our battles and struggles with sin. That's why the Bible is called the *"Sword of the Spirit"* in Ephesians 6:17. Paul goes on in verse 18 to urge us to

"...be alert and always keep on praying for all the Lord's people." God knew we were going to struggle, even with taking care of our bodies, but He gave us a way to fight. And he expects us to use it. We can't just throw in the towel because it's hard to put away our own fleshly desires. We are called to put what we want, our desires, last and what God wants first. Oh, that we would get to the place where we can genuinely pray that His desires become our desires.

Because of all this, we should be training our bodies physically, spiritually, mentally, and emotionally. We should be striving for a clear mind to better hear the Lord, healthy body to serve the Lord, stable emotions to minister on behalf of the Lord, and spiritual readiness to learn continually from the Lord and share the Gospel of the Lord. It's all about the Lord. I am not a doctor, and it's super important that you speak with your doctor before making any drastic changes to diet or lifestyle. So, what have I learned about taking care of my body?

I have three autoimmune diseases which have caused me to adhere to a very strict gluten-free, dairy-free, hormone and antibiotic-free, nightshade vegetable-free, processed-free diet. Yes, I realize I sound like a freak. And, in absolutely no way, am I telling you to eat like me. I only do it because I have to. There are, however, several things I have learned about healthy eating that, had I known earlier in life, may have spared me from the autoimmune issues I have today. Autoimmune diseases that get in my way.

I'll try to keep this simple. Feel free to do your own research. The first thing you need to know is that the FDA has basically approved many ingredients to go in our foods that are junk. Unhealthy junk that can cause a plethora of health problems, including cancer. Ever wonder why people were not so sick back when our grandparents and great grandparents were young? It's because they were not eating the processed foods that we eat today. Do your thirty, fifty and seventy-year-old self a favor and try to limit your consumption of processed foods as much as possible. Another thing I have learned? They pump our meats with hormones and antibiotics. Why is this so bad? The hormones that are put in our meats trigger endocrine disrupters, meaning they disrupt the normal process of our endocrine system, which produces and regulates our hormones. And, the antibiotics that are put in our meats can cause our bodies to become resistant to antibiotics. Crazy but true. Remember, we are not to be slaves to anything, and this includes our food. We have got to pray for self-control concerning how much we eat. Pray for God to give you discernment about when you should stop eating. Don't become enslaved by your food. Moderation is everything when it comes to being healthy with our bodies. This includes moderating sugar, gluten and other parts of our diet that may not be bad until we are in the habit of having too much.

Along with what we put in our bodies, there are several things we should not put in our bodies. Now, I'm not going to give you the whole speech on smoking because surely by now everyone reading this knows that smoking causes cancer anywhere in our bodies, not just our lungs. It causes COPD, other respiratory diseases, stroke and coronary heart disease, damage to our blood vessels, clots and blockages, vision problems, autoimmune issues and, believe me, the list goes on and on.[31] I used to joke that the number one thing I learned in nursing school was that smoking causes everything. I think I've shared enough for you to know that it is a very harmful sin that holds us captive and ruins our lives. Don't smoke.

Now, I'm not going to join the debate on whether or not drinking alcohol is a sin. That is not my intention for bringing it up. Jesus turned water into wine and drank it at the Last Supper – yada yada yada. We can debate until we are blue in the face. Being a slave to alcohol is a sin, however, because, once again, we are not to be slaves to anything. If drinking it causes you to become enslaved by it, stay clear away from it at all cost because it will not only ruin your health but also your family, your relationships, and, ultimately, your life. Alcoholism causes liver damage, pancreatitis, a weakened immune system, and cancer, of course. Another important point to bring up about alcohol is this: if you are around people who struggle with alcohol or drinking too much of it, you should stay away from it, too. Paul gives clear instructions for this in 1 Corinthians 10:31-33:

So, whether you eat or drink or whatever you do, do it all for the glory of God. Do not cause anyone to stumble, whether Jews, Greeks or the church of God -- even as I try to please everyone in every way. For I am not seeking my own good but the good of many, so that they may be saved.

Millions of people are struggling with alcoholism. Don't be their stumbling block.

We've talked about what to put in our bodies and what not to put in our bodies, but there are other lessons of physical health I wish I had learned a whole lot earlier. Get some sleep. Get it now. I know, I know. Late nights studying or even hanging out with friends are inevitable. And, sleep gets much harder after you have kids. No matter the phase we're in, we have got to learn to lose sleep in moderation. If you only get three hours one night, be sure to schedule in a long nap the next day or get an extra couple of hours the next night. Sleep is so important! Being sleep deprived not only causes the obvious "grumpy gills" attitude and loss of concentration, it also weakens our immune system, raises our blood pressure, increases our risk for accidents and diabetes, affects our ability to remember, and sets us on a downward spiral concerning endocrine health. I used to boast about what I could accomplish after only a few short hours of sleep – until it all caught up with me years later. Why couldn't I have learned this one earlier? Get some sleep, and a lot of it.

While physical health is super important, we, as a church, have ignored the importance of mental health. Depression is real. Anxiety is real. Eating disorders, personality disorders, panic disorders, compulsive disorders, phobias, PTSD, among many others, are real. And mental health is a huge part of our physical health. It is all related. We, as church girls, have got to stop assuming people with depression are sad because something is wrong with their relationship with Jesus. Or, that people with anxiety need to just give it all to God, so they won't be so anxious. This is no truer than telling someone who has just had a heart attack that it wouldn't have happened if they read their Bible every day. Just like we see a cardiologist for heart issues or a nephrologist for kidney issues or an endocrinologist for thyroid issues, we must seek the appropriate help for our mental issues. Ignoring it is doing no one any favors.

If you think you might be struggling with some of these problems or disorders, please don't ignore it. Don't wait for it to ruin your relationships, career, and, eventually, your life. Also, if you do not struggle but know someone who does, don't ignore them either. Help them. Encourage them. Walk alongside them. Love them. While most mental health disorders are not exactly preventable, there are some things we can do to foster mental health. Be sure to see your primary care physician regularly and be honest about any issues you are having. Try to live a healthy and active lifestyle. Find ways to destress and do them often. What works for one may not work for someone else. And please, please, if or when you become pregnant, keep all toxins, alcohol, smoke and drugs away from your body and your baby's body. Mental health is serious, and we cannot ignore it anymore. And, don't let the church tell you otherwise.

Resolve in Your Heart

You only get one body. Taking care of that body demands intentionality, and it's better to head down the path least traveled while you're younger. When Judah was taken into captivity by King Nebuchadnezzar of Babylon, the king ordered that Israelite men who were young, handsome, smart, wise and qualified be brought to serve in the king's palace. Daniel was among these young men. He and his friends (Shadrach, Meshach, and Abednego) were to be trained in the culture of the Babylonians, and one of the perks of serving in the king's palace was being able to eat the king's food and wine. But, Daniel resolved in his heart that he would not defile his body with the king's unclean food. He made a choice, and then he stuck to it. You probably know the rest of the story. Daniel and his friends ate their clean food and the rest of the young men ate the king's food. At the end of ten days, Daniel and his friends were stronger and healthier than the others. Now, can we take this remarkable story of Daniel and learn that eating healthy is important, and we will be better because of it? Absolutely. But I also want us to learn an important concept that, if applied, could change our lives. Daniel made a choice. Daniel resolved in his heart. He didn't wait until he tasted the king's food to make his decision. He didn't decide while he was under the influence of the king's wine. He didn't even pray about what to do because he already knew it was against God's law to eat the king's food. Daniel made a choice before he was in the middle of temptation that he was not going to eat the food. Church girls, whether it's overeating, not eating enough, alcohol, smoking, constantly staying up late, or being lazy, we must resolve in our hearts today the kind of life we want to live. Decide now what you believe about keeping your temple healthy and make a plan for how you are going to live it out.

Church Girls, I can't possibly write enough about this topic in one chapter, but, if you only take away one thing from this chapter, let it be this. God loves you and wants to use you for His glory and purpose. How we take care of our bodies matter. Do what you can now, when you're young, to create healthy habits to set you up for a future ready to serve Jesus in whatever capacity He calls you. After all, this is the purpose of our existence.

Your health actually matters,

Holly

Make it Stick, Church Girl

1. Have you ever been guilty of trying to add something to Jesus? Food? Friends? Success? Workouts? Explain.

2. Are there habits you have now that may hinder you from serving Jesus to your fullest potential later? Explain.

3. In what ways have you potentially been a stumbling block to someone else?

4. Mental health is often ignored in the church. Do you know someone who is struggling with a mental health disease? What are some ways you can encourage, and how can you be intentional about not ignoring it?

5. Write a prayer asking God to show you things you need to give up or things you need to add to your lifestyle to be prepared for Him to use you.

Dear Church Girl,
It's Okay to Be a Woman

I had to give my daughter "the talk" at an unusually early age. Let's just say they learn way too much, way too fast in school these days. But nonetheless I gave her just what she needed to know and explained why it was so important that we do it God's way. Several weeks later, she very randomly looked up at me and said, "Momma, I'm not EVER getting married cause I don't need a man." She then went on to inform me she didn't want a baby coming out of her "you know what" and so she was going to have to adopt anyway. So, I guess she's right. There really is no need for a man in her plans. I'm so grateful she has an independent spirit and wants to be able to take care of herself. It really is one of my favorite things about her. But sometimes I cringe, just a little bit, at the thought that she would become callous toward men, that she might be swept away by this newer "feminism" movement we know today.

What is Feminism Anyway?

Let me explain myself. Feminism has changed over the years, a lot. When you read the definition of feminism, Merriam-Webster's Dictionary says it is "the theory of the political, economic, and social equality of the sexes."[32] And this is great! We live in America and every one of our citizens should have equal rights no matter their sex, race, ethnicity and so forth. Thank the Lord for women like Susan B. Anthony who played an important role in women's suffrage and many others like Madeline Albright and Sandra Day O'Connor, who showed the world you don't have to be a man to help lead a nation. I am one hundred thousand percent for equal rights for women - equal pay, equal status, equal job opportunities, and all that jazz.

The problem is the only type of feminism that is getting a buzz is very liberal or radical feminism. You know the no bra, free bleeder, hate men, no make-up, women should take over the world kind of feminism. Our media has a play day with it, and that seems to be the only feminism that makes it on our news feed and social media.

The She-Woman Man-Hater Club

Have y'all ever seen *The Little Rascals*? It's a darling movie about a group of boys who enter a soapbox car race. They are also part of this club called the He-Man Woman-Hater club, and they vow to never love girls. The only problem is that Alfalfa, a member of the club, falls in love with Darla, a cute little girl, which goes against all the club rules. I won't ruin the rest of it in case you haven't seen it, but it is hilarious. All joking aside, radical feminism has created its own She-Woman Man-Hater Club.

This new culture is telling us that the only way to truly support women is to hate men. And we hate them by trying to be more like them. It's ironic, huh? Radical feminists lean on the ideas that women are better, not equal, and that men should be less than, not the same. Radicals believe that all men are out to get them and want to take over the world in some kind of male supremacy patriarchy. I'm not at all denying that there are many men who would love for the white male to take over the entire world, but what I am saying is that it is not the vast majority. At least not here, in America. How do I know? I live in the South. As you probably already know, the South has a false reputation of male supremacy. You know, the women should be barefoot in the kitchen, raisin' the kids kind of culture. But that's not really how it is. I can honestly say I've lived in the South for over thirty years now, and I do not even personally know any men like this, not that there aren't any. But, ladies, it is definitely not the majority, so why in the world is it all of a sudden popular to hate men? It's almost viewed as humanitarian these days.

Allow me to explain a little bit about me and my personality. I'm a doer. I do have goals and am a bit of a visionary, but I'm a "Let's get the work done" kind of girl. I have often been accused of trying to do what men might more naturally do just to prove that I can do it. But, honestly, I just want to get the job done. And, if I don't need a man to get it done, why should I go get one? I have a very strong, dominant, and independent personality that some may argue is less than feminine. The other day, I carried the pieces to my daughter's new desk up the stairs to her room. This was no kids desk, and we clearly didn't pay attention to the size because it barely fit in her room. Oops. After carrying all the pieces upstairs, making sure all the hardware was accounted for, and getting my hammer and Philips screwdriver, I began to assemble the desk. It took about four hours from start to finish, probably average for that size of desk, but then it came time to put the top on the desk - the very huge desk. I yelled for my man. He came upstairs, helped me lift the top to mount to the body, replied, "Looks good, Babe," and then went back downstairs. I didn't assemble the desk myself to prove a woman could do it. I'm the daughter of a builder, so my husband already knew I could assemble the desk and didn't mind me doing it. I actually enjoyed it! When I needed help, I got my man.

I hope this illustration provides some balance to this whole issue. I may not need a man to do most things, but I certainly don't hate them or view them as less-than. The truth is, I'm cheering for men. I want them to do great things, follow God's plan, and succeed in life. And not because I need them to, but because I love them and want them to succeed. These are our fathers and brothers and eventually our husbands and sons! Why are we not cheering for their success along with the success of women? Which brings me to another point.

The Next Generation of Men

Another problem of radical feminism is the message it is sending to boys and young men. Now I know this book is primarily for young women, but just hear me out because this does directly involve you. Our recent culture has been teaching our boys and young men to be scared and ashamed of being a man. They are trying to strip away their "manly" qualities or hobbies and shaming them for possessing something that is natural to their being. Now, let me be clear what I mean by "manly" qualities or hobbies. These would be things like strength, assertiveness, competitiveness, protectiveness, provision, or hobbies like sports, hunting, etc. Now let me be clear what I do NOT mean by "manly" qualities or hobbies. These are things like violence, reckless behavior, woman shaming, giving in to impure sexual impulses, etc. These are not traits, these are sins. While having manly qualities and hobbies doesn't make you a man, it certainly is not wrong for men to possess them. But, unfortunately, our society has been telling our boys and young men that having those qualities is wrong, conveying that they shouldn't be assertive or competitive, that they shouldn't want to be the protector. You know, because we are all supposed to be the same, right? But, ladies, these are your future husbands we are talking about! Think about it. Would you want to grow up and marry someone who wasn't absolutely sure that he is a man and that he is okay with being a man?

Jesus and the Woman

Now that we've established what radical feminism is and the dangers that can come with it, let's take a look at the role women play in the story of our beloved Jesus. First of all, Jesus valued women. One time, Jesus stopped in the streets to address not just a woman but a woman with a serious medical issue. This was highly unusual for a man to do, especially in public. Another time Jesus defended a woman who was sleeping around and about to be stoned, and He did it publicly. In front of the Pharisees! And, yet another time, Jesus stopped and even talked with a Samaritan woman who was viewed as unclean, to share the Gospel with her. Jesus never let culture dictate the way He valued or loved women.

We also see many times throughout Scripture where Jesus not only valued women but valued a woman's place in His ministry. Remember when Jesus visited Mary and Martha? Martha was up cleaning house and cooking dinner, but Mary was sitting at Jesus' feet, learning from Him. Jesus didn't say, "Mary, get in the kitchen, woman." Instead He said, *"Mary has chosen what is better, and it will not be taken from her"* (Luke 10:42).

Jesus wanted Mary to further her education and learn all about the Savior, even if she was a woman. In fact, Jesus involved several women in His ministry. Check out what Luke has to say.

After this, Jesus traveled about from one town and village to another, proclaiming the good news of the kingdom of God. The Twelve were with him, and also some women who have been cured of evil spirits and diseases: Mary (called Magdalene) from whom seven demons had come out; Joanna the wife of Chuza, the manager of Herod's household; Susanna; and many others. These women were helping to support them out of their own means.
Luke 8:1-3

These women, Mary Magdalene, Joanna, Susanna, and even the ones not named were helping to support Jesus and the disciples. They were ministering to them. They were acting as deaconesses to Jesus. And, he is quick to point out that they were doing it out of their own means. Because they wanted to. Because they loved Jesus and believed His message. Why do you think Luke feels the need to point that out? I believe it is so our generation would know they were not submitting to Jesus as a woman was forced to submit to a man. They were submitting to Jesus out of a genuine desire to serve Him and His cause. Women were important to the ministry of the most important person ever to live, both historically and Spiritually. And we are too, ladies!

It gets better. After Jesus' death, He was buried (prepared by women, I might add) and rose victorious three days later. The women came to the tomb and found that no one was there, and the angel of the Lord told them that Jesus has risen! The women met Jesus and saw Him with their own eyes. He spoke to them and instructed them to go and tell the disciples. John tells us:

Mary Magdalene went to the disciples with the news: "I have seen the Lord!" And she told them that he had said these things to her.
John 20:18

Jesus used a woman to be the first one to proclaim His resurrection, something that would turn the world upside down! Wow. No one will ever convince me that Jesus is not pulling for women too and that He does not long for us to be used by Him. Women are important to Jesus and His ministry.

What About That Proverbs 31 Chick?

Oh, our beloved, yet purposely forgotten, woman from Proverbs. Do you feel sorry for her? Do you strive to be her? Do you envy her? I mean, how does she do it all? Most look at this woman from Proverbs with contempt. The expectation is too high. And, where in the world is the husband anyway? What is he up too? Because she seems to be the one doing all the work. She's also viewed as a homemaker who hand-makes all the Halloween costumes, grows her own pesticide-free food, and is president of the PTA. What we often fail to see, however, is the strength and devotion of this woman to things outside the home. Get cozy, cause we are gonna camp out here for a while.

A wife of noble character who can find? She is worth far more than rubies.
Her husband has full confidence in her and lacks nothing of value.
She brings him good, not harm, all the days of her life.
Proverbs 31:10-12

Clearly, this woman means a lot to her man and is valuable to him. He is confident in her. Why? Well, first of all she's not out to get him or hoping that he doesn't succeed because he's a man, and she's certainly not off trying to find someone else. She doesn't harm him or his reputation and is good to him until the day she dies. Clearly, she wasn't a radical.

She selects wool and flax and works with eager hands.
She is like the merchant ships, bringing her food from afar.
She gets up while it is still night; she provides food for her family and portions for her female servants.
She considers a field and buys it; out of her earning she plants a vineyard. (v. 13-16)

Calm down. This is not telling us that we should be sewing all the clothes for our entire family - or their Halloween costumes. During the time Solomon wrote this, the best quality of clothing was what was made at home. Bless our hearts, this is just not the case in our culture today. This woman is eager to be sure her family is dressed in nice clothing, not expensive, but nice. She is eager to teach them dignity based on how she dresses them. Allow me to elaborate for a moment. When we dress immodestly or inappropriately, we are stripping layers of our dignity. Many liberal feminists today believe that we have the right to dress however we choose and show whatever we want because we have that right as women. But sisters, we don't have that right as Jesus followers. Let's be eager to dress with dignity and teach our daughters to do the same.

This girl also makes sure her family is fed. She went on shopping trips and traveled however far she needed to in order to buy food for her family. Now, I know I don't travel far, but my grocery trips to Walmart, Whole Foods, and Aldi in one day have got to count for something, right? She's not lazy and gets up early enough to make sure her family has breakfast. And, yes, I'm sure cereal counts. She also is organized and delegates tasks to her female servants (those who work for her).

And then she goes to work. You heard it right. She goes to work. She can't consider a field without actually going to the field. She works outside the home as well. Ladies, you need to hear me loud and clear. The Bible never tells us that we are to stay at home. Yes, we are to care for and work within the home, but here we read that we absolutely can work outside the home as well. And, we can be successful. This woman not only buys a field, but she plants a vineyard. She is going to profit from it, which also means she is smart with her money. Yes, you heard right again. Her money. Money she earns. Get it, girl!

She sets about her work vigorously; her arms are strong for her tasks.
She sees that her trading is profitable, and her lamp does not go out at night.
In her hand she holds the distaff and grasps the spindle with her fingers.
She opens her arms to the poor and extends her hands to the needy. (v. 17-20)

We can obviously assume this woman is taking care of herself. She is strong and able to work energetically. She sees her day job has been successful but doesn't just come home and collapse. Instead she works until late at night. How is she able to do this? Because she is taking care of herself. She has the energy and strength to finish the laundry or do the dishes or plan the next day. She also takes care of others. She ministers to them. This may seem like an awkward place to mention ministering, but I think it's intentional. I believe she is also staying up late ministering. Late night counsel sessions, preparing her small group lesson, or practicing music for worship. Ministry happens after hours, after a day at school or the office, after homework or making dinner, and sometimes even after showers and brushing our teeth. Whatever way she is ministering, she is probably doing it in what little free time she has.

When it snows, she has no fear for her household; for all of them are clothed in scarlet.
She makes coverings for her bed; she is clothed in fine linen and purple.
Her husband is respected at the city gate, where he takes his seat among the elders of the land.
She makes linen garments and sells them and supplies the merchants with sashes. (v. 21-24)

This lady is clearly not a procrastinator. She is prepared for any situation, even snow. She's not only prepared for the snow. She's prepared in style, and she's lookin' fly. She takes pride in her appearance and the appearance of her house. And, why do you think Solomon is all of a sudden mentioning the success of her husband? Isn't this about the noble woman? I think this is also intentional. Her husband is respected and successful because of all the previous verses we read. You've heard the expression, "Behind every good man is a great woman." But, based on what we read here, she is not behind him but beside him, working hard, doing her thing, and basically killin' it. Her success is his success.

She is clothed with strength and dignity; she can laugh at the days to come.
She speaks with wisdom, and faithful instruction is on her tongue.
She watches over the affairs of her household and does not eat the bread of idleness. (v. 25-27)

A few days ago, I found my very first gray hair. I admit, I was devastated. I called my husband into the bathroom to make sure I wasn't seeing things. Upon confirmation, I quickly pulled it out. Trust me, young ladies, I wasn't laughing. But this woman is laughing. I imagine it's more of a chuckle. "Bring it on," she says. She knows the Word of God because we are told she is wise and faithful to instruct. She organizes everything that goes on between her people and has never heard of lazy.

Her children arise and call her blessed; her husband also,
and he praises her:
"Many women do noble things, but you surpass them all."
Charm is deceptive and beauty is fleeting; but a woman
who fears the Lord is to be praised.
Honor her for all that her hands have done, and let her
works bring her praise at the city gate. (v. 28-31)

What is it about this woman that her husband, children, and even city praise her? It's not the fact that she hand-makes clothes, home cooks every meal, is involved in real estate, manages the success of her family and looks good while she does it. Nope. She is praised because of the womanly qualities she possesses. Qualities such as a strong work ethic, energy, wisdom, compassion, confidence, and dignity. The kind of qualities that make others stop and take notice. The entire city is fascinated by her. Why are these qualities so appealing? Because these qualities don't make us weak, they make us strong, exceptional, smart, successful, prepared, and even attractive.

Why am I spending so much time on this married woman with kids when you probably have just recently crossed the threshold of womanhood? Because I want you to know it's okay to be a woman. Own it. God's Word, our ultimate authority, very clearly paints a detailed picture of what a woman ought to be, and she's killin' it. Why in the world would we not want to embrace this? Please don't listen to what society is telling you about this topic.

Me, Too

I know many young women reading this have had tragic experiences with men, whether it be from strangers, family, friends, or even church staff. Some have been treated unfairly at their workplace and are trying to cope with a long history of sexual harassment. Some are stuck in verbally and physically abusive relationships. Some have been sexually abused from childhood, leading to devastating consequences. If this is you, I want you to know that we hear you. We see you. We stand with you and hurt for you. We don't blame you or question you. We don't ignore you. And, we stand in the gap for you.

Diane Strack, founder and president of She Loves Out Loud ministries, is passionate about gathering women to pray in the gap between trauma and triumph, anger and peace, and bitterness and forgiveness. In a speech given at the Capitol in Washington D.C., Diane vows that "we will love unconditionally, we will listen intently, we will serve and we will earnestly pray because love is not silent. Neither are we."[33] Young women, we will stand in the gap for you. And, we will not be silent.

A Woman's Place

So, what is it that He's called you to do? What is your place in the home, in society, and in the church? Believe it or not, feminism can be healthy. Let's look back at Webster's definition of feminism: "the theory of the political, economic, and social equality of the sexes."[34] By this definition, everyone should be a feminist because women should be equal. But may I suggest that equal and alike are not the same. I know that's a confusing sentence, so allow me to elaborate.

Women are equal to men. We read in Genesis that *"God created mankind in his own image, in the image of God he created them; male and female he created them"* (Genesis 1:27).

Both men and women are equally created in the image of God. Galatians 3:28 tells us, *"There is neither Jew nor Gentile, neither slave nor free, nor is there male and female, for you are all one in Christ Jesus."* Based on the authority of God's Word (and, it is the ultimate authority), we are equal participants in the work of Jesus Christ. We all have the same value and worth in our political, economic, social and spiritual arenas of our world. But does this make men and women alike? Sure, we have things in common with men, but for the most part, we are quite different. Let's take a look at why women were created to begin with.

The Lord God said, "It is not good for the man to be alone. I will make a helper suitable for him."
Genesis 2:18

Did you catch that? The man needed help. I find it hysterical that women were created because men couldn't do it without us. God could have created another man. In fact, He could have only created men. But more men was not what man needed. The Hebrew word for suitable is "to put in front of, in view, part opposite."[35] This had to have been intentional. My husband can't find anything in the refrigerator if it's not put right in front of his face when he opens the door. I guess God wanted to make sure he could find her. But God created something different enough to notice and put her in front of his face, because our differences help. As women, our differences help our families. Our differences help our government, schools, churches, and planet. If we are longing to be the same as men, then our world would still be led by men alone - only men with boobs. And, doesn't this defeat the point of feminism? We should not be striving to be like them. We should be striving to take advantage of our differences and help. Where do we help? We help wherever God calls us to help. Some of you reading this haven't figured that out yet, and that's okay. God has always called you to help in the home. Help your husband and help raise your kids. Your place may be in the kitchen, but it may also be in the Supreme Court. God may call you to help other kids or minister to the next generation of youth like He has me for the last 15 years. Your place may be to help take care of the sick by becoming a nurse, doctor, or neurosurgeon. God may call you to help create or build infrastructures in your community by becoming an architect, a contractor, or a builder. God may call you to help disciple others by becoming a Bible teacher. Your place may be to help your country by becoming a U.S. Congresswoman or even the

President. God may call you to help strengthen the economy of your town by owning a business. The opportunities are limitless - almost. There is one thing I'm sure of. God is not calling you to be a man, and it is not your place to be like a man either.

All My Single Ladies

Don't lie. You totally just sang the title of this section. Me too. But that's exactly who I'm speaking to here, all the single ladies, which may be most of you. You need a man. You need a man who will always be there for you. You need a man who will protect you, help you, encourage you, love you, and who would lay down his life for you. Single lady, the only man you need is Jesus.

I make an extra effort with my own daughter to make sure she knows this. Sure, we will teach her to change a tire, handle her finances, and use basic tools. We want her to know how to take care of herself without a man. Why? We don't know what God has in store for Annabeth's life. Will she be a candy taster, which is the desire of her eight-year-old heart? Maybe. But she may be a missionary overseas. She may join the military. She may be a worship leader. She may be the one to find a cure for cancer. She may be the next President. And, she may be a stay-at-home mom raising the next generation's warriors in God's army. But what we want Annabeth to know is that she doesn't need a man to accomplish what God calls her to. She needs Jesus. She needs to seek Jesus. She needs to long for Him and commit to Him. And, so do you.

Commit to the Lord whatever you do, and he will establish your plans.
Proverbs 16:3

It's true. Sure, we need men for some things, especially that whole makin' a baby thing, but you don't need a man in your life. You only need Jesus. I have been happily married for 16 years and never once have regretted getting hitched. I love my man and, frankly, couldn't imagine life without him. But I did not marry him because I needed him. Wanted him? Yes. But I only needed Jesus.

And my God will meet all your needs according to the riches of his glory in Christ Jesus.
Philippians 4:19

Trust in the Lord and do good; dwell in the land and enjoy safe pasture. Take delight in the Lord and he will give you the desires of your heart.
Psalm 37:3-4

It's a beautiful place to be when we surrender our plans over to the One who holds the universe and allow Him to be our everything. Church girls, marriage is amazing. Having a man by your side, ministering together, and raising a family are wonderful things I am privileged to be a part of. But I do not need these things. And, neither do you. Seek Jesus, and He will establish your plans, whatever that may be.

For Such a Time as This

And who knows but that you have come to your royal
position for such a time as this?
Esther 4:14

Young women of God, we are royal. As daughters of the King, we have a royal position. I believe that we have this royal position for such a time as this. A time when our culture is lying to us about who we should be. A time when our society tells us our worth is wrapped up in how we look or how much income we make. A time when radical feminism is challenging us to hate men and only love ourselves. Who knows but that we have been given our royal positions for such a time as this? A position that compels us to demand better for our daughters, nieces, and next generation of women. A position that causes us to speak the truth of King Jesus and that our worth is rooted in the redemptive crown we wear, not the size of our dress or the mascara on our face. A position that encourages us to come alongside our men and fight the war this society has declared on us.

Will we be brave for our King or bow to fear of our culture? Will we be fierce for the Gospel or indifferent of our faith? Will we bear the Truth with confidence or shrink in the shadows of the lies? Church girls, we were bestowed this royal position for such a time as this. King Jesus, give us courage to proclaim the truth of Your Word to a broken world. Give us wisdom to know our worth rests in Your righteousness. Give us endurance to fulfill Your mission.

King Jesus, use us, Your royal women, for such a time as this.

Instead of trying to do everything that men can do, let's try to do what God has called us to do. When we forsake the calling God has for us as women, we are saying our plans are better than God's plan. Sister, His ways are higher and bigger and stronger and way better than what we can imagine.

Now to him who is able to do immeasurably more than all we ask or imagine, according to his power that is at work within us, to him be the glory in the church and in Christ Jesus throughout all generations, forever and ever! Amen.
Ephesians 3:20-21

He can do immeasurably more than whatever dreams or goals or hopes we can come up with in our finite minds. But if we are going to be used in this God kind of capacity this verse speaks of, we have got to stop trying to beat the man. It's okay to be woman. In fact, it's great!

It's okay to be a woman,

Make it Stick, Church Girl

1. Has someone in your life ever made you feel less-than because you are a woman, or have you experienced something in your life that has made you a man hater? Explain.

2. What thought first came to mind when you thought about the Proverbs 31 woman? Have your views of her changed after reading this chapter?

3. What qualities from the Proverbs 31 woman do you struggle with the most?

Pray over these. Ask the Lord to help you focus on the attributes of this noble woman and not her to-do list.

4. Is there a verse in Scripture about women that you struggle with? Explain.

5. Read 1 Corinthians 7:32-35. What do these verses teach us about being single?

Let's learn to be concerned with the affairs of the Lord before we concern ourselves with the affairs of man.

Dear Church Girl, You're Already Dead

It was such a fun day, magical really. It was a day filled with fun rides, amazing food, exciting parades, beautiful princesses and Mickey Mouse. It was an unforgettable family vacation. My kids got the experience of a lifetime that week with surprises and indulgences that seemed endless. We decided to end one of our days at Downtown Disney (now known as Disney Springs). There is one place at Downtown Disney that was and still is a family favorite: Goofy's Candy Shop. The build-your-own chocolate covered rice crispy Mickey heads are not only delicious but also fun to watch as they are being made. This particular night, we decided to also get chocolate covered strawberries. For the life of me, I cannot remember why we got chocolate covered strawberries, but I do remember one thing -- we had to share them. We bought 6, and there were 5 of us. You can do the math. There was one chocolate covered strawberry left over. My son, Jaxon, who was 3 ½ at the time asked for the last strawberry. We told him he would have to share. He was not happy about this, and the whining began. It was clear to us that he felt entitled to that treat, so because of his attitude, we told him that he could not have any part of the last chocolate covered strawberry. And then it happened. The loudest, most blood curling scream from my boy. "I just wanted a strawberry!" People stared. Not only that, people stopped and stared. The judgmental looks from other parents and families were piercing. We all froze and stared at each other. It. Was. Mortifying. To everyone but my mom, that is, who stared with us and then turned around and began to laugh, trying to hide the fact that she still thought he was just the cutest thing ever. How could someone who had been given the opportunity to do so much and have so much fun pitch a fit over sharing one chocolate covered strawberry? I know the answer, although at the time, I could care less about the answer and more about finding a hole to hide in! Jaxon was lost in his own little world. He did not care about his parents, who had paid for such a magical trip. He did not care about Mamaw, who took time off work to come on vacation with us. He did not even care about his little sister, who was just barely pushing two years old at the time. He did not care about the hundreds of other families who were trying to enjoy their time at Downtown Disney. He didn't even care that Mickey Mouse, himself, could be watching him throw this atrocious fit! All he cared about was Jaxon and what Jaxon wanted. He was making the vacation and family time all about him. Now, you might be thinking, "Oh, he was just 3 ½ years old. He didn't know better and has to learn." And, that's my point exactly. It is natural as sinful human beings to want it to be all about us and to feel entitled, and some would even call it normal behavior, especially for young people.

No Excuses

Psychology will teach us that it is normal behavior for a young person to have a narcissistic perspective on life for this phase of adolescence. Dictionary.com defines narcissist as "a person who is overly self-involved, and often vain, and selfish."[36] While society might view this as "normal," I challenge you to see this for what it really is -- sin. Take a look at what the apostle Paul has to say about this in his letter to the believers in Philippi:

Do nothing out of selfish ambition or vain conceit. Rather, in humility value others above yourselves, not looking to your own interests but each of you to the interest of others.
Philippians 2:3-4

Jaxon had absolutely no interest in others that night at Downtown Disney. He was only looking to his own interests. We do the same thing, almost daily. It's like when someone pulls out in front of you or cuts you off in the elevator. They are looking out for their own interests. Paul goes on to say we should have the same mindset as Jesus:

Who, being in very nature God, did not consider equality with God something to be used to his own advantage; rather, he made himself nothing by taking the very nature of a servant....
Philippians 2:6-7

Despite what society would have us to believe, Christians have been called to be servants, no matter our age. Church girls, listen up! You do not get a free pass to make it all about you because of what psychology, science, or society says about you. They may say you are supposed to act entitled and selfish because you are young, but God's Word tells us something different. No excuses. James 3:16 warns us:

For where you have envy and selfish ambition, there you find disorder and every evil practice.

I can't think of a better way to describe my high school years than "disorderly," and my social circles were certainly consumed with "evil practices." Hatred toward those who were different, disrespect for authority, drugs, alcohol, sexual immorality, just to name a few. One thing they all have in common? They were practiced because of selfishness. Maybe we think of ourselves as better than those who don't look or act like us, so we harbor hatred and anger toward others. Maybe we wanted to escape the horrible life we have or just wanted to fit in, or just wanted to feel good, or just wanted to prove we were mature enough, so we started a downhill spiral of illegal drugs or alcohol or sexual immorality or all three. Maybe it's not that "big" for you. Maybe you treat your parents with disdain because you think they owe you the world, and you're entitled to it. Maybe you are angry with your professor because you expect to get a good grade even though you didn't work for it or angry with your coach because you've missed half the practices and had to sit on the bench. Maybe you are losing friends because you constantly make life and conversation about you. It's not about us. Paul has a lot to say about this in 2 Corinthians 5:15-17:

And he died for all, that those who live should no longer live for themselves but for him who died for them and was raised again. So from now on we regard no one from a worldly point of view. Though we once regarded Christ in this way, we do so no longer. Therefore, if anyone is in Christ, the new creation has come: the old has gone, the new is here.

Wow. I love how something that was written two thousand years ago can still be so completely relevant to us. We are called to no longer live for ourselves, just because the world says it's normal. We are a new creation. It doesn't say, "You will be a new creation when you're 25, since the years before are so difficult" or "The old will go away and the new will come once you reach your late twenties and society expects you to grow up a little." We have got to stop with the excuses. Once you surrender your life to Christ and make Him Lord of your life, a new creation has come and is here! Young women, stop using your age as an excuse, or you will miss out on what God has called you to do! Oh, the years I wasted because I did not learn this sooner. I don't mean to step on your toes. Or I do.

You'd think that this is just something you outgrow, a phase so to speak. But believe it or not, it's a lifestyle that is no respecter of age.

Lifestyle of an Entitled Nation

Ahh, the American Dream. It's the goal of every natural born citizen and the hope of many peering from beyond our borders. There is a certain drive in most Americans, Christians included, to succeed and accomplish goals. A desire to "keep up with the Jones's" so to speak. We usually have a relative picture of how we want our lives to go, even from a very young age. We want a great job, a big house, nice cars, and vacation time. And when we achieve this, we believe we must be doing something right. Surely God would not bestow such blessings and benefits if we were not pleasing Him, right?

But, that's not what we read from Amos. If you are not familiar with this book, it is a difficult read. It seems that you are just reading about the doom and gloom of Israel over and over again in each chapter, and, if we are not careful, the relevance of the book gets lost in the pages. And remember, God's Word is always relevant. Every single part of Amos had a purpose for Israel in 760 B.C. and has a purpose for us in the 21st century.

At this point in history, Israel has been divided into two kingdoms, Judah and Israel. Both kingdoms are prospering economically and financially. Both militaries are strong and all seemed to be well. You could say that they were living the American Dream. They must have been doing something right to have been given so much prosperity, right? Well, not so, actually. That's why God sent Amos, the prophet, to announce judgment on them.

In the entire first and part of the second chapters, Amos announces the sins of several different pagan nations and the judgments God will bring on them. He says because Damascus threshed Gilead with sledges having iron teeth, God will send fire and consume their fortresses. He says because Gaza took captive whole communities and sold them to Edom, God will send fire on their wall and destroy their king. He goes on to state the similar fate for Tyre, Edom, Ammon and Moab. Can you imagine what the Israelites must have thought of this announcement from this not-so-well-known prophet? I can just hear them say, "Yeah, set fire to all them pagan nations, God! They get what they deserve! Go get em'!" To hear only the sins and judgment of their enemies would have been pleasant to their ears! They were probably thinking, "Boy, this Amos is the best prophet ever!" That is until he continued. In the rest of chapter two, Amos lists the sins of Israel and Judah. And their list is longer than the sins listed for the pagan nations. Their list includes rejecting the law of the Lord, not keeping His decrees, being led astray by false gods, selling the innocent for silver and the needy for a pair of sandals, trampling the poor, denying justice to the oppressed, father and son using the same girl, and lying on the altars of false gods (Amos 2:4-8).

Now, isn't this a lot like us? We think because we do the whole church thing, attend college Bible study, and listen to Hillsong radio that we must be doing enough to please the Lord. I mean it is all about us, right? Clearly our sins of gossiping or cheating or watching that one rather questionable Netflix show go unnoticed because of all that we actually do, right? And, obviously we church girls are entitled to have the Lord's favor because of it. This was the exact attitude of God's people we read about here in Amos.

Imagine their surprise to hear their nation, God's people, among the pagan nations with a list of sins far longer than the other nations. Remember, this is a time in Israel's history of idolatry, indulgences, immorality, corruption, and oppression of the poor. What do you think was the point of listing the sins and judgments of the other nations? God was trying to tell them that they were no different. Just because they had plenty of undeserved blessings and benefits, did not mean God was pleased with them. The next several chapters of Amos focus on two things. God reminds them of how He has remained their faithful provider since delivering them from Egypt, and He tells them the details of what will happen to them if they don't repent.

And that's what Amos calls for them to do in chapter five. He continually tells God's people to repent and to *"Seek the Lord and live...perhaps the Lord God Almighty will have mercy...."* (Amos 4:6,15).

Do you know that God's judgment and mercy are always together? They go together like PB & J. Like milk and cookies. Like Chick-fil-A sauce and waffle fries. All joking aside, God's judgment and mercy are always together. But we tend to dwell only on the judgment. God is announcing His judgment but also pleading with Israel to seek Him so that they may live and possibly be spared this awful wrath. He is calling them to stop living their own way and follow His way. Stop fulfilling their own agenda and fulfill His. Stop making it all about them and make it about Him. Stop making their own plans and surrender to His plans -- all so they may truly live.

What does this have to do with us? How is all this doom and gloom, repent or perish stuff relevant to us church girls? I'm so glad you asked. Let's take a look at chapter six, where Amos begins by saying:

Woe to you who are complacent in Zion, and to you who feel secure on Mount Samaria.
Amos 6:1

The dictionary defines complacent as "showing smug or uncritical satisfaction with oneself or one's achievements."[37] It defines secure as "not subject to threat and certain to remain or continue safe and unharmed."[38] And do you know what "woe" means? It's defined as great sorrow or distress."[39] So, what God is warning here is basically that great sorrow and distress will come to those who show smug satisfaction with themselves and to those who are certain they will remain safe and unharmed. Ladies, this sounds eerily familiar. It sounds exactly like the entitled society in which we live. If we continue reading in Amos, we see some other striking similarities.

You put off the day of disaster and bring near a reign of terror. You lie on beds adorned with ivory and lounge on your couches. You dine on choice lambs and fattened calves. You strum away on your harps like David and improvise on musical instruments. You drink wine by the bowlful and use the finest lotions, but you do not grieve

over the ruin of Joseph. Therefore, you will be among the first to go into exile; your feasting and lounging will end.
Amos 6:3-7

Alright, so I know we do not sleep in beds made of ivory, and most of us probably don't consider lamb as a top choice for dinner. And, who in America still plays the harp, right? But allow me to possibly put a modern twist on this. Today we may say we lay in our rooms inside our nice houses with flat screen TV's, Joanna Gaines décor, and jetted tubs. And we lounge on our leather couches with reclining seats sitting in front of our fancy fireplaces or yet another flat screen TV all complete with Netflix, Hulu, Cable, Amazon Prime, Xbox, PlayStation, and Disney Plus, of course. All while we indulge in our favorite snacks and food including deluxe pizzas, filet mignon, macaroni and cheese, Krispy Kreme donuts, homemade ice creams with every topping imaginable, and Starbucks. We play our music and entertain ourselves using our new iPhones, iPads, MacBook's, or Alexa, Pandora, Sirius XM, and Spotify...putting in our ear buds and ignoring the fact that we are ignoring God. We drink our clean, filtered water, our lattes and Frappuccino's, our ice-cold Cherry Cokes and sweet tea. And, we use the best smelling lotions, body washes, shampoos and conditioners to put on our freshly cut balayage hair. We indulge in all these things and more, only to become comfortable, complacent, and proud. Too proud to seek God. Too proud to surrender our plans and ideas. Too proud to let Jesus rule on the throne of our hearts. Too comfortable to live differently for Him. Too complacent to care about our own souls let alone the souls of others. Too self-seeking to give our lives wholly and completely over to Jesus Christ.

But God warns them that their feasting and lounging will end. And it did end for Israel. The judgment of Israel that was prophesied by Amos came to fruition about thirty years after Amos spoke those God-inspired words. Israel was taken captive by Assyria. And, about one hundred years later Judah was taken captive by none other than King Nebuchadnezzar of Babylon. Sound familiar? What's completely ironic is the fact that Judah was taken captive by a nation who is known, biblically and historically, for their indulgent lifestyle. We learn about it in history but also read all about it in Daniel. Isn't it ironic that God would allow them to be taken captive by a self-indulgent, complacent and secure nation?

But God, through Amos, tried to warn Israel that their feasting and lounging would end. And it will for us too. There will come a day when none of this will matter at all. The houses, the cars, the entertainment, the money, and the drama will not matter. Our luxuries and indulgences will not matter. Our physical security or strong army will not matter. And even the American dream along with the Jones's will not matter. All that will matter is: Did we make it about Christ? Did we seek Him? Did we surrender to His plans? Did we allow Jesus to rule over our life? Did we seek Him with our heart?

But then we get to the final chapter of Amos. Remember what I said about judgment and mercy always being together? The end of chapter nine describes the mercy that is coming. I absolutely love when the Old and New Testaments collide to tell the beautiful, redemptive story of the Messiah. That's what's happening here. Amos is prophesying about the Messiah coming to restore all things and restore every nation that bears His name. Christ, God's only Son, was sent to rescue us from our sin. Knowing we were sentenced to death because of our sin, Jesus died in our place, bearing our sin. Three days after He was buried, Jesus rose to conquer the grave, so we can one day do the same! And He will return on this same day to restore Israel and restore all the nations and people who bear His name.

There's only one thing Israel was told to do. Repent. You see, repentance leads to restoration. Restoration is being made new. Isn't that what Jesus does for us? He makes us new. He turns these dirty rags into a beautiful wedding gown as we unite with Christ. We are His bride. And He made me new when I chose to surrender my life to Him over 20 years ago, and now I can come before the throne of God with no condemnation but dressed in the righteousness of Jesus. And you can be made new, too. Jesus can restore you, too. If you are reading this and want to know more about how Jesus can restore you, put a bookmark in this chapter and read the *I Was but Now* section at the end of this book.

Many of us are living our indulgent lives so focused on our own comfort and happiness that we are ignoring God's call for us to repent. But our feasting and lounging will end. There will come a day when we will either get to experience restoration in full or we will get to experience death for the rest of eternity. Seek God and live! Mercy triumphs over judgment when we choose Jesus!

So, What's It About Anyway?

Humanitarianism is cool. It is definitely the "in" thing right now. We need to save our planet and feed the hungry. The other day, I was walking into Target with my eight-year old daughter (probably to get a Starbucks drink we felt entitled to), and she said, "Mom, I ate with the boys at lunch today." This was definitely something weird for her to say, so I asked her about it. She replied, "Because all the other girls are VSCO girls." Why in the world did my eight-year-old know about VSCO girls? I questioned, "Annabeth, what's a VSCO girl?" Using very dramatic hand motions, she replied, "Ya know, like 'scrunchies' and 'save the turtles' and stuff. Can't we just eat our lunch? I'd rather play soccer." Priceless. Now, while I do try to limit our use of plastic, I have nothing against scrunchies, and goodness knows a good canteen makes all the difference, I was rather relieved that my daughter wasn't quite ready to label herself. She's perfectly content just being Annabeth.

Nevertheless, humanitarianism is all the rage right now. And, I am in no way discouraging you to be a humanitarian. We all should care about these things and do what we can to help. I do, however, want to challenge you to look at what's going on around you. You see, we often only want to make humanitarianism about recycling and saving animals and helping those in crisis across the globe. While there is certainly nothing wrong with doing these things, we need to remember what's right in front of us. There are ways to better the human race, and they're right outside our doors. Sometimes we are so stuck in our own little world that we are completely oblivious to what is going on around us, whether it be the lonely girl at school who needs a friend, the barista who has been blessed out by the third customer, the elderly lady at church who just needs a smile, the exhausted mom who needs help watching her kids, your parents who need you to pull your weight around their house, the younger sister who needs a good example, or the friend who actually needs you to speak truth into her life. Ladies, I can think of no better way to better humanity than to speak and show them the love of Christ. To do this, to notice these opportunities, we have got to stop making it about us.

Once we are able to realize life is not about us or our agenda, and we are not entitled to any of it, only then can we fully grasp what it's really about or, rather, who it's really about. Church girls, as Jesus followers our purpose in life is to glorify the Lord and point others to Him. That's it. That's our purpose. And, while it is the same goal for all believers, it looks different for everybody. Our hobbies, careers, responsibilities, and mission fields are all different, giving us different avenues to glorify Jesus and share the Gospel. And, you know what, ladies? One day we will be held accountable. It's not something we like to talk about, but we will. Did we make it about Jesus? Did we allow God to use us for His kingdom plan? Or, did we make it about us? Did we live our lives with an attitude of entitlement to live it our way?

Jonathan Evans, a former NFL athlete, Chaplain for the Dallas Cowboys, brother to author/speaker Priscilla Shirer, and son to pastor/author Dr. Tony Evans, preached at his mother's funeral service. He spoke of how he wrestled with God after she passed away. He questioned why God would not answer their prayers for victory over cancer and show His glory, only to lose the wrestling match and the Lord to reveal the victory his mom had received. But it was in this message that he also addresses the issue of entitlement we have as God's people. He said the Lord answered him as such:

> I appreciate your prayers and trust in me. But the way you are coming at me right now is with a sense of entitlement like I owe you something. You can't tell me what I'm supposed to do. I'm God....Don't come to me with that entitlement. Because without my victory and what I have done, all of you would be on the doorsteps of hell. I don't owe you anything. You owe me everything.[40]

It's easy to see how we are living with an attitude of entitlement concerning our occurrences with others in our everyday life, but do we also see it in our relationship with the Lord? How are we approaching His throne concerning His plan for our lives? Are we coming at Him with a sense of entitlement as Jonathan Evans would suggest? Are we coming expecting Him to fulfill our wishes and give us our demands? Are we approaching His throne like 3 ½ year old Jaxon and the chocolate-covered strawberry?

You're Already Dead

A couple of weeks ago at the start of the new year, my pastor, Dr. Sam Greer, preached a message on anticipating what God is going to do. He told us the story of missionary James Calvert, who was called to take the Gospel to the cannibal islands of Fiji. While sailing to the islands the captain of the ship urged them to turn around, for they would surely die. Calvert replies, "We died before we came here."[41]

This. What a beautiful and overwhelming picture of what it means to surrender to Christ. What Calvert is referring to is found in Galatians 2:20, which says, *"I have been crucified with Christ and I no longer live, but Christ lives in me"* and also Colossians 3:2-3, which says, *"Set your minds on things above, not on earthly things. For you died, and your life is now hidden with Christ in God."* When we surrendered our lives to Christ, we chose to die to ourselves. When will we get to the place where we can be okay with being dead to ourselves and alive in Christ?

Church girls, we were created to serve the purposes of an almighty God who does not need us for anything yet died for us anyway. We owe Him our plans, our goals, our schedules, our dreams, our present and future. We owe Him our careers, our families, our hobbies, and our finances. We owe Him everything because we are already dead. Let's step out of our own little world and allow ourselves to be used for the purpose we were created for, even as young women. I think the Lord will open our eyes to opportunities all around us.

You're already dead,

Holly

Make it Stick, Church Girl

1. What are some ways you tend to "make it all about you"?

2. What global crisis or agenda are you most passionate about?

3. What opportunities to make it about Jesus have you passed up this month?

4. Has God revealed ways you have been putting in your earbuds and ignoring Him?
Explain.

5. Was there ever a time that you approached God with an attitude of entitlement?

6. List some specific areas you need to change in order to make it about Jesus and His plans instead of your own?

The Gospel

I Was but Now

Hey, church girl! I just have to tell you about these grapes. They're called Holiday Grapes and are quite possibly the best thing you've ever put in your face. Ok, at least the best fruit you've ever put in your face. They are huge but not too fleshy, and when you bite down on them, they explode in your mouth like one of those gushers you used to eat when you were a little kid -- or the gushers that you still eat now as a big kid -- no judgment here. And they are the sweetest grapes you've ever tasted. Anyways, I tell everyone about how good these grapes are, and, if I'm in public, I will pass them out for all to try because they are that good and everyone should know about these wonderful things! People look at me like I'm a crazy person (which, I realize, is debatable) when I offer them a grape. But after they try it, they get this look in their eyes. Their face says, "Oh, it makes perfect sense now why you have offered me this grape because this truly is the best grape I've ever had." And then they ask for another one, which usually ends in me getting a different kind of look in my eye. My face says, "You experienced for yourself how good they are, now why would you abuse my grace by asking for more?" And then I usually give them another one -- only because it's the nice thing to do. The point is that these grapes are so good, I just can't help but share. There is something else in my life that is oh, so good, and I must share it with you -- something much more meaningful and satisfying than these grapes.

Have you ever wondered what your purpose is here? Have you ever thought, "What is the meaning of all this, anyway?" Church girl, I have the answer. The creator of the universe wanted to have a relationship with us, and that is why we were created. Let that sink in -- that someone so mighty and powerful did not have to create us and did not even need to create us, but actually wanted to create us. Why are we here? We exist to be in relationship with God and glorify and honor our Creator! God has a perfect plan for us and has had one since the beginning of time. But, of course, we think we know better and head off in a different direction, creating our own plan. We call that sin, and we ALL do it. Walking away from God's plan causes us to be broken. We try to fill that brokenness with things like relationships, money, drugs, violence, bitterness, and careers, among others, but it never satisfies us and leaves us broken and longing for purpose. In middle school, I was filling this brokenness with boys, attention, self-gratification, and popularity. And, my actions and attitude showed such. My momma said she could not stand me when I was in middle school because I was disrespectful, arrogant, and just plain mean. What she thought was just middle school normalcy turned out to be a lost church girl trying to fill the void, a void that left me still broken.

But here's the good news! God loves us so much that He sent a solution to our problem, someone to fix our brokenness and bring us back to God's perfect plan. God sent His Son, Jesus, to pay the penalty for our sin. God's Word tells us that *"...without the shedding of blood there is no forgiveness"* (Hebrews 9:22), so God sent His absolutely perfect Son to die on a cross in our place, bearing our sin. What love! Our debt has already been paid, but it's up to us to accept it by asking Jesus to forgive our sins and choosing to follow His way.

But it doesn't just stop there. God did not just provide forgiveness of sins and a better way for our life on earth but also after death as well! You see, after Jesus died for our sins, He was placed in a tomb. He was there, lifeless, for three days. But then it happened. Jesus rose from the tomb, defeating death, and lives forever. What does this mean for Jesus followers? God's Word tells us in Romans 6:5 that since *"We have been united with him in a death like his, we will certainly also be united with him in a resurrection like his."* Even after this life on earth, God promises us life eternal through His Son, Jesus. What grace!

When I was in eighth grade, I realized what I needed to fill that void and make myself new, or, rather, who. I needed Jesus. I didn't just need to know about Him. I didn't just need to hear others preach about Him. I didn't even just need to sing about Him. I needed a relationship with Him. I needed to personally know Him, and I needed to make

Him Lord over my entire life. On a Sunday night in September, I asked the Lord to forgive my sins and surrendered my life to Him. Choosing to be forgiven of our sin and choosing to follow Jesus puts us back on God's perfect plan for our lives. No, it doesn't mean that life will be perfect, but it means that we serve a perfect God who will give us the satisfaction and joy we can find nowhere else. So, even in the midst of our pain or stress or hurt, even in the midst of the chaos life throws at us, we glorify a merciful God who has made a way for us to be in a real relationship with Him, a relationship that can grow and flourish. It's a relationship that can be nourished by talking to Him, worshiping Him, reading His Word and engaging in a community of other believers!

You know those grapes I was telling you about? There is one big problem with them. They are temporary. These wonderful grapes are only sold September through January. I guess that's why they're called Holiday Grapes. So, February through August I am left longing for them, a desire which will not be satisfied until the next September. But I will have Jesus forever. He doesn't ever go away or leave me, even when life is chaotic and messy. I am always satisfied with Jesus, my Savior. He loves you so much, church girl. He wants you so much. It's what you were created for, and He is the purpose of life that you have been searching for. Do you know Him?

P.S.

I certainly did not write this book because I have it all figured out. Because I don't. At all. Every day is a living testimony of God's grace on my life. It really is sufficient, ladies. Through all our failures, hurts, mess-ups, sin, chaos, and second-guessing, the Lord's grace is sufficient for us, and He is ultimately glorified.

My grace is sufficient for you, for my power is made
perfect in weakness.
2 Corinthians 12:9

I wrote this book for three reasons.

God told me to write. It was clear and unmistakable. While parents might not be able to get away so easily when we ask "why" and they respond, "Because I said so," God can. He can say so, and we have no right to question. He is so big, and His plans are so vast, there is no way for our finite minds to understand His completeness. He told me to write this book, and I don't think I will ever know all the reasons why. But He has beautifully orchestrated a plan for our lives and the way He wants to use us. Isn't it refreshing to know that He has the plan and not us? It's only up to us to be willing and obedient.

I believe the Word of the Lord empowers us. No one can give you power outside of the Holy Spirit, which is why this book is saturated with Scripture. I long for women to know the Word of God and let it empower them. Empower them to live in truth and not fear. Empower them to be strong in their faith. Empower them to serve. Empower them to fulfill God's purpose for their lives. When we know the Word, love the Word, and live the Word, we are empowered.

I am not alone. There is no way on God's beautiful green earth that I am the only church girl who has struggled like this. Struggled with my prayer life. Struggled with my identity. Struggled to be kind and forgive. Struggled to know the Word and actually make it stick. I know there are so many more just like me. I wanted to share my story in the hope that the Lord will take this book and put it in the hands of other women who struggle, so they know they're not alone. So, they can be encouraged. So, they get practical, real-world advice based on God's Word. And, so they can maybe -- just maybe -- learn from some of this before they are entangled deep in the weeds of adulthood.

I pray these letters challenge you to examine your life. I pray these truths help equip you to be a doer and not just a hearer. I pray they inspire change and are shared with others. It's time to make it stick, church girl.

—

[1] Brent Crowe Ph.D., sermon at Student Leadership University.

[2] Theodore Roosevelt, "Quote Fancy" https://quotefancy.com/quote/33048/Theodore-Roosevelt-Comparison-is-the-thief-of-joy. Retrieved 21 January 2020.

[3] Abbott-Smith, *A Manual Greek Lexicon of the New Testament,* electronic ed. (2014), s.v. "eklegó."

[4] Abbott-Smith, s.v. "hierateuo."

[5] Abbott-Smith, s.v. "hagios."

[6] Oswald Chambers. *My Upmost for His Highest* (Grand Rapids, MI: Discovery House, 1992), September 1.

[7] Abbott-Smith, s.v. "eis."

[8] Abbott-Smith, s.v. "aggelos."

[9] Abbott-Smith, s.v. "elegcho."

[10] Abbott-Smith, s.v. "anorthoo."

[11] Abbott-Smith, s.v. "paideuo."

[12] Delight. 2020. In *Dictionary.com*. Retrieved 21 January 2020 from https://www.dictionary.com/browse/delight?s=t.

[13] Anonymous.

[14] C.S. Lewis, "Quote Fancy"
https://quotefancy.com/quote/781222/C-S-Lewis-Prayer-in-the-sense-of-petition-asking-for-things-is-a-small-part-of-it.
Retrieved 21 January 2020.

[15] Sophie Bethune, 2014. *Teen stress rivals that of adults*.
American Psychological Association. Retrieved on 21 January
2020 from https://www.apa.org/monitor/2014/04/teen-stress.

[16] Wes Ford, Sermon at Red Bank Baptist Church. 2019.

[17] Forgive. 2020. In *Dictionary.com. Retrieved 21 January 2020
from https://www.dictionary.com/browse/forgive?s=t*.

[18] Lewis B. Smedes, "Quote Fancy"
https://quotefancy.com/quote/758944/Lewis-B-Smedes-To-forgive-is-to-set-a-prisoner-free-and-discover-that-the-prisoner-was. Retrieved 21 January 2020.

[19] *How Holding Grudges Can Shorten Your Life & How to Move
On*. 2019. Neurocore: Brain Performance Centers. Retrieved 21
January 2020 from
https://www.neurocorecenters.com/blog/holding-grudges-can-shorten-life-move.

[20] Ibid.

[21] Messias E, Saini A, Sinato P, Welch S. 2010. *Bearing grudges
and physical health: relationships to smoking, cardiovascular
health and ulcers*. NCBI. Retrieved on 21 January 2020 from
https://www.ncbi.nlm.nih.gov/pubmed/19387519.

[22] *Histamine.* 2017. Encyclopedia Britannica. Retrieved 21 January 2020 from https://www.britannica.com/science/histamine.

[23] Erick Raymond, *Common Questions Christians Ask About Forgiveness.* 2018. The Gospel Coalition. Retrieved 21 January 2020 from https://www.thegospelcoalition.org/blogs/erik-raymond/common-questions-christians-ask-forgiveness/.

[24] *The Preacher's Outline and Sermon Bible: Vol. 1* (Leadership Ministries Worldwide, 2017), 391.

[25] "DISC profile" https://www.discprofile.com/what-is-disc/overview/. Retrieved 31 March 2020.

[26] Kindness. 2020. In *Lexico by Oxford.* Retrieved 21 January 2020 from https://www.lexico.com/en/definition/kindness.

[27] Abbott-Smith, s.v. "chrestotes."

[28] Brent Crowe Ph.D.. *Chasing Elephants: Wrestling with the Gray Areas of Life* (Colorado Springs, CO: NavPress, 2010), 37.

[29] J. Strong, *Strong's Concise Dictionary of Bible Words*, electronic ed. (Thomas Nelson, Inc., 2000), s.v. "checed."

[30] Robby Gallaty, sermon at Youth Ministry CONCLAVE conference. Chattanooga, TN. 2020.

[31] Kerry H. Cheever and Janice L. Hinkle. *Brunner & Suddarth's Textbook of Medical-Surgical Nursing* (Hong Kong: Wolters Kluwer/Lippincott Williams and Wilkins, 2014).

[32] Feminism. 2020. In *Merriam-Webster's Dictionary.* Retrieved 21 January 2020 from https://www.merriam-webster.com/dictionary/feminism.

[33] She Loves Out Loud. *Diane Strack shares the vision of http://shelovesoutloud.org.* Online video clip. YouTube. 8 May 2019. https://www.youtube.com/watch?v=F5Jmctw_D1o. Retrieved 22 January 2020.

[34] Feminism. 2020. In *Merriam-Webster's Dictionary.* Retrieved 21 January 2020 from https://www.merriam-webster.com/dictionary/feminism.

[35] Strong, s.v. "neged."

[36] Narcissist. 2020. In *Dictionary.com* Retrieved 21 January 2020 from https://www.dictionary.com/browse/narcissist.

[37] Complacent. 2020. In *Lexico by Oxford.* Retrieved 21 January 2020 from https://www.lexico.com/en/definition/complacent.

[38] Secure. 2020. In *Lexico by Oxford.* Retrieved 21 January 2020 from https://www.lexico.com/en/definition/secure.

[39] Woe. 2020. In *Lexiso by Oxford.* Retrieved 21 January 2020 from https://www.lexico.com/en/definition/woe.

[40] Tony Evans. *Dr. Lois Irene Evans – A Celebration of Life and Legacy.* Online video clip. YouTube. 8 January 2020. https://www.youtube.com/watch?v=FGxsa8vLU4Y. Retrieved 21 January 2020.

[41] Sam Greer Ph.D. Sermon at Red Bank Baptist Church. 2020.

About the Author

Holly Ford is a fellow church girl from Knoxville, Tennessee, who was born practically wearing her Sunday best. With a father, grandfather, and three uncles who were preachers, Jesus and His church have always been the biggest part of Holly's life. She has been a follower of Jesus since the age of eleven and has now been a student pastor's wife for more than 15 years. Holly currently lives in Chattanooga where her husband, Wes Ford, serves as Student Pastor. They have two very active and outgoing children, who are a lot of things, but boring is definitely not one of them. Holly began blogging with the intention of encouraging other women in the faith. Soon, she felt God calling her to teach His Word. She began to pray for the Lord to give her a desire for Scripture and that it would become her delight. He answered abundantly, giving Holly a passion for not only knowing His Word but allowing it to empower her to fulfill His purpose for her life. Holly's passion is to minister to women through writing, Bible study, and speaking and to encourage them to know God's Word and let It empower them.

Connect with Holly

Instagram: @_holly_ford

Facebook: Holly Ford

If you are interested in Holly speaking at your next event, visit

HOLLYFORD.ORG